Gartner

56 Top Gallant Road
P.O. Box 10212
Stamford, CT 06904-2212

Multisourcing

Multisourcing

MOVING BEYOND OUTSOURCING TO

ACHIEVE GROWTH AND AGILITY

Linda Cohen

Allie Young

Gartner, Inc.

HARVARD BUSINESS SCHOOL PRESS

Boston, Massachusetts

Library of Congress Cataloging-in-Publication Data

Cohen, Linda, 1953-
    Multisourcing: moving beyond outsourcing to achieve growth and agility /
Linda Cohen, Allie Young.
        p.   cm.
    Includes index.
    ISBN 1-59139-797-9
    1. Contracting out—Management. 2. Industrial management. I. Young, Allie,
1950– II. Title.
HD2365.C64 2006
658.4'058--dc22

                                                                    2005013878

Contents

Acknowledgments   vii

introduction
Moving Beyond Outsourcing   1

one
A Map to Multisourcing   17

two
Prepare for a Well-Aligned Sourcing Strategy   35

three
Build Your Sourcing Strategy   65

four
Govern and Manage Multisourcing   111

five
Evaluate and Select Service Providers   143

six
Negotiate Your Contract   171

seven
Measure Your Progress   193

conclusion
The Multisourcing Imperative   215

Appendix   223

Notes   231

Index   235

About the Authors   243

Acknowledgments

As with all research at Gartner, this book is the product of the dedicated work of many people. First we want to thank the many clients we've worked with over the years. We've learned as much from them as they have learned from us, we're sure. We especially want to thank those who spent a considerable amount of time with us and gave us permission to use their stories to help others: Bert Dumars at Nike, Ken Hill at General Dynamics, Chris Jones at Qualex, Mark Nelson at IndyMac Bank, Dietmar Reiner at Ontario Power Generation, Grant Reusch at Sun Microsystems, Bob Ridout and Maryann Holloway at DuPont, and Barbara Scarcella at Thomson.

Above all, everything we have presented in this book is a result of, and based on, the collaborative research done in conjunction with the global team of Gartner analysts and consultants since the early 1990s. These analysts and consultants continue to be the backbone of Gartner's sourcing research content, thought leadership, and point of view. Some examples of their work are noted in the text, but even those mentions do not capture sufficiently their contribution to this book. The effort of these individuals allows Gartner to undertake major sourcing conferences each year; without these people, we could not even contemplate a project like this. We sincerely thank each of them and acknowledge them for their contribution to, and support of, Gartner's sourcing research and practice.

We'd especially like to note the incalculable contributions of Denise Underwood, who stepped in toward the end of the project and helped guide the last several chapters of the book. Without her in-depth knowledge of sourcing practice, commitment, aid, and review, the book would be a shadow of what it is; it certainly wouldn't have such good case studies! Others who deserve mention for spending considerable amounts of their own time on the text, making sure we got everything right, include Chris Ambrose, Cassio Dreyfuss, Rich Matlus, Bill Maurer, and Lorrie Scardino. Additional significant contributions to content were made by Marianne Broadbent, Rob Brown, Roger Cox, Claudio Da Rold, Fran Karamouzis, Ellen Kitzis, Arnaud Klerx, Jim Longwood, Jim Murphy, Kevin Parikh, Martin Stacey, and Lisa Stone. Finally, Jennifer Beck, Rich Cockcroft, Stacy Hawkins, David Howe, Bob Patton, and Eric Rocco deserve mention for creating the space needed for an effort like this project.

In terms of actually creating this book, the first person we want to thank is Tim Ogden, our resident editor. There simply would not have been a book without Tim. He was simultaneously the catalyst for new approaches to communicating ideas and the voice of reason to keep the focus on the business intent and business outcomes of Multisourcing as a discipline. Tim's clear-minded counsel guided the entire process, from the book's inception through publication, and helped transform Multisourcing principles, theories, and content into actionable advice. We sincerely thank him for the long hours that he spent to perfect and influence every sentence of this book.

Finally, when we started *Multisourcing,* we had no idea of the scope of background effort required to make any book a reality. Therefore, we want to thank some key individuals who shouldered that background work with little or no recognition: Susan Barry, our agent, and Heather Levy, formerly the publisher of Gartner Press, both of whom helped us kick things off before moving on to other projects; Tom Hayes, group vice president of public relations and a significant sponsor of the project; William Bangert and David Churbuck, both of whom contributed immensely to developing the content and structure of *Multisourcing*; and Jacque Murphy, our editor at Harvard Business School Press, who had enough faith in this project to look past the early stumbles and to work with us to see it to the finish line.

Moving Beyond Outsourcing

Multisourcing: the disciplined provisioning and blending of business and IT services from the optimal set of internal and external providers in the pursuit of business goals.

O UTSOURCING WORKED. USING EXTERNAL SERVICE providers to cut costs and improve performance has become truly commonplace. As much as the popular press has focused on the debate over the benefits of outsourcing, no executive leadership team, board of directors, or government agency of any size would deny that outsourcing is a vital, even integral, part of successful operations today. Wall Street and other international capital markets certainly agree. Surveys show that companies that announce plans for outsourcing routinely see share price growth; CEOs who outsource see their compensation increase.[1] Economists will tell you that the cost savings and efficiencies associated with outsourcing have been a major factor in corporations' ability to control costs and maintain profitability despite extreme cost pressures since the 2000 downturn. There is no question, outsourcing has worked.

But precisely due to this success, new challenges are emerging. The high expectations associated with outsourcing are increasingly hard to meet. As more and more functions are outsourced, integrating and managing a portfolio of service providers is becoming more difficult—and is causing significant service disruptions in many organizations.

Large outsourcing services companies are coming under pressure from capital markets to grow revenues and generate predictable margins. And, of course, outsourcing to cut costs no longer provides significant competitive advantage—all your competitors are using outsourcing as well and are reaping the same cost advantages. As a result of all these pressures, our research shows that fully 50 percent of outsourcing contracts signed between 2000 and 2004 will fail to meet expectations.

Before continuing, we should take a moment to clarify terms. In this book, we are discussing services outsourcing, *not* manufacturing outsourcing. These two are very different animals, and they require very different management approaches. Even within the world of services outsourcing, however, there is significant misunderstanding of what outsourcing actually is. Outsourcing is contracting with an external firm for the *ongoing management* and delivery of a defined set of services to a prescribed level of performance. Key to this definition is the concept of the ongoing management of services by the external firm. Outsourcing is not simply hiring contract workers or short-term, project-based work provided by third parties—what is often referred to as staff augmentation or body shopping. Outsourced services may be provided domestically, that is, on-site (in the enterprise's own buildings) or off-site (at the outsourced service provider's site). Alternatively, outsourced services may be provided nondomestically, that is, offshore or nearshore (at the outsourced provider's site in another country or a country adjacent to where services will be delivered). Therefore, outsourcing does not always mean sourcing services from other countries, although this is how the term is often used in the popular press.

The Way Forward

GIVEN THAT achieving strategic advantage via outsourcing is becoming increasingly difficult while expectations for success continue to be very high, how can we move forward? What can you do to ensure the success of your outsourcing initiatives—to use outsourcing to create competitive advantage, to improve your growth prospects, and to increase your agility in responding to changing circumstances? The way forward requires, somewhat paradoxically, that you abandon thinking about outsourcing in and of itself and adopt a more holistic and strategic approach to sourcing as a whole.

"This is not a supply chain opportunity to delegate or dump costs. It is a chance to use partnerships to augment skills, to scale a fast-growing business, or to provide capabilities for competitive advantage," notes Dick LeFave, CIO of Nextel, a provider of wireless communications services, which announced plans to merge with Sprint in 2005.[2] The question of what functions and services a company should build and provide for itself, versus what it should seek from the outside world, is at the heart of a decision process that can mean significant improvements to a company's profitability, agility, customer satisfaction, and competitive posture.

The way forward requires a new approach that goes beyond outsourcing as it has traditionally been viewed. It requires that the selection of the "right" sources for business services—whether internal or external—be an integral part of enterprise strategy. It requires identifying the desired business outcomes and creating contracts, relationships, measurement, and governance that support and enable those outcomes. This new approach is what we call *Multisourcing*, a new operational model that obtains business services from multiple sources inside and outside corporate walls to obtain the best business outcomes. Or to put it more formally, Multisourcing is the disciplined provisioning and blending of business and IT services from the optimal set of internal and external providers in the pursuit of business goals. To implement Multisourcing, a new operating model must be adopted, including new approaches to sourcing strategy, sourcing governance, sourcing management, service provider selection, and service measurement. Although most organizations by default employ an array of partners, service providers, and internal resources, few realize the strategic importance of blending internal and external providers in achieving business goals like agility and growth. Multisourcing must be embraced, developed, managed, and continually refined in an organization. The rewards of doing so can be enormous. Consider the example of DuPont and a global manufacturing and services company (which we'll call GMS), which have applied a Multisourcing approach to an increasingly large part of their operations.

Agility has been an absolute necessity for DuPont. In less than a decade, the company has seen more than $60 billion worth of investments, acquisitions, joint ventures, divestitures, and dissolved partnerships as it reshapes its business to compete in global markets. This figure is even more stunning when you consider that it is nearly two times larger than DuPont's annual revenues. The only way for DuPont to effectively provide information technology (IT) and other services in such a dynamic environment is through Multisourcing. DuPont has created what it calls a global IT alliance that blends services from more than ten service providers and DuPont's own internal resources to meet the demands of the business. "Providing high-quality service in such a rapidly changing environment would be impossible using only internal staff," says DuPont's CIO, Bob Ridout. Maryann Holloway, director of the IT alliance, says that integrated management is key to delivery: "We have to maintain positive partnerships with our service providers, and they have to work well with each other, so that we can all jointly meet changing needs."[3]

GMS, on the other hand, has used Multisourcing disciplines to drive dramatic cost reductions in business process services like accounts payable. GMS's accounts-payable process has in fifteen years moved from being highly centralized and internal, to globally decentralized and internal, to globally decentralized with a mix of internal and external resources. "The reason we've been able to manage such change while delivering effective services and cutting costs is that we have invested heavily in governance and management capabilities internally, while integrating our service providers seamlessly into those processes," says Claire White (a pseudonym), global VP of business services.

How Did We Get Here?

To understand the way forward, it's useful to look at how we have arrived at our current state—the need to move beyond outsourcing to Multisourcing. The current wave of the outsourcing of services can't be traced to any particular source, but a number of significant events and developments have served to amplify and reinforce it.[4] One of these seminal events occurred in 1991, when the concept of core competency was first advanced by management strategy consultants Gary Hamel and C. K. Prahalad in a *Harvard Business Review* article, "The Core Competence of the Corporation." Hamel and Prahalad sparked a period of introspection by corporate leaders on the essential question "What business am I in?" The success of many CEOs in shedding subsidiaries and business functions led to the rise of the "cult of core competency," and along the way, outsourcing—its decades-old heritage notwithstanding—came into its own as a path toward streamlining a corporation down to its essential elements.

The cult of core competency was reinforced by another significant management theory in the 1990s, put forth by James Champy and Michael Hammer in their book *Reengineering the Corporation.* Following the lead of Champy and Hammer, organizations studied in detail many of their business processes to find ever more efficient ways of carrying them out. Armed with this knowledge of process and frustrated by the difficulty of generating real performance gains, many executives followed reengineering to one of its logical conclusions: outsourcing processes to external providers that could perform them more efficiently.

On the back of core competency and reengineering, outsourcing swept over management theorists and practitioners in the 1990s, inspiring a revolution in corporate structure that continues today. The incredibly rapid economic growth the late 1990s and the sudden crash of the early 2000s only reinforced the wave. In the rapid-growth phase at the inception of the Internet-based economy, many organizations experimented with outsourcing in an effort to accelerate time to market, manage growth, and gain access to hard-to-find and expensive skills. During the downturn, outsourcing leaped to the fore as a cost-saving quick fix when budgets came under pressure. Soon every element of a corporation's IT and business operations was potentially up for outsourcing consideration.

We should also mention the reinforcing impact of technology and communications advances. Beyond the Internet, the availability of increasingly cheap computing power, storage, and communications bandwidth has meant that services never previously outsourced are now regularly delivered by external service providers. Take call centers as just one example. Not too long ago, every company had its own batch of operators taking calls. Advances in computing power and storage capacity ushered in computer-telephony integration—allowing automated resolution to more calls and enabling human operators to handle far more callers. At the same time, the plummeting cost of communications bandwidth means that calls can be diverted to a central location where one external service provider can answer calls for hundreds of companies with a small group of operators. Huge savings have been commonly realized by organizations that have capitalized on these newly available services.

The net result of all these factors has not just been a largely successful (for all parties) explosion in outsourcing, with the overall services outsourcing market reaching three-quarters of a trillion dollars in annual revenue by 2008.[5] It has created a "cult of outsourcing" every bit as powerful as the cult of core competency that led to a decade of reengineering and downsizing. Today, many organizations and executives pursue outsourcing almost compulsively. Every service in the organization is considered a candidate for outsourcing, even without any evaluation, benchmarking, or consideration of future impact. These organizations and executives vastly underestimate the complexity of managing and integrating multiple outsourcers. Often they treat the outsourcing of even the most critical services as simply a procurement exercise—lowest bid wins, with no consideration of the ability to deliver.

Compulsive outsourcing has also been driven by globalization. The entry of global competitors into so many markets has accelerated the need to seek competitive and especially cost advantages—outsourcing seems the only alternative. Similarly, the drive to rapidly build a presence in some of the world's fastest-growing markets such as India, China, Brazil, and Russia has caused many organizations to use outsourcing to ramp up quickly.

This compulsive outsourcing—outsourcing for cost reasons without integrated planning, strategy, and ongoing management—has masked the rapidly changing complexity of the services outsourcing world. Organizations are often giving the same level of attention to hiring an outside company to run the corporate cafeteria, or a landscaping service to mow their lawn, that they give to outsourcing the highest levels of their research and development efforts. While services outsourcing is not by any means a new phenomenon, for much of its history it has been primarily focused on discrete services such as the cafeteria, building maintenance, basic infrastructure, and the mail room. In these cases, managing outside suppliers was relatively simple—there is no chance that grass clippings will end up in the sandwiches or that meatloaf will show up in someone's inbox. The realm of services that can be outsourced, however, has grown exponentially and now includes many integral parts of an organization's workflow. These services both support and depend on any number of other workstreams in the organization. When the grass is not being mowed, the source of the problem is obvious. When a significant project fails to meet a deadline because key contracted personnel don't deliver, because the outsourced finance organization hasn't paid invoices, because the outsourced HR provider's personnel tracking systems were down, because the outsourced IT organization's systems were not functioning properly, who is to blame?

At the same time that we have become plagued by compulsive outsourcing, the market for services is changing rapidly as well. Outsourcing companies are driving to standardize their services so that these companies too can grow rapidly while keeping costs under control. This has often created huge tensions between the expectations of service recipients and the needs of service providers.

What's the Problem?

The experiences of so many firms show that the current state of chaotic and compulsive outsourcing creates as many challenges as it solves. And the problems are most often not with the external provider; they lie within the organization itself and in the shortcomings in their sourcing practices: miscommunication, misalignment, poor governance, and a lack of coordinated management. Take, for example, the experiences of these three clients that called us for help after their own outsourcing experiences led not to lower costs or improved performance but to wasted effort and misspent dollars.

Miscommunication

A large global manufacturing company decided to outsource all its IT support services to a global provider.[6] After nearly a year of research, due diligence, and negotiation, a five-year exclusive contract was signed. The firm's CIO promised the board that the deal would cut IT support costs by 15 percent per year. Three months into the deal, the company completed the acquisition of a competitor that had major operations in Taiwan. Suddenly, the CIO's staff began receiving frantic calls: "Our users in Taiwan can't get any support. No one at the help desk speaks the Taiwanese dialect of Chinese!"

The CIO later discovered that the acquisition of the competitor had been in process for some time, but the acquisition plan had not been shared with the CIO or the contract negotiation team. The outsourcing contract was drafted and signed with a vital piece of information missing. The original contract specified all the languages the service provider had to provide support in; the Taiwanese dialect was not among them. In fact, the service provider had no employees who spoke the Taiwanese dialect at all. The CIO entered another round of negotiations over a barrel: with the exclusive five-year contract already in place, the service provider had all the leverage and could pass on all the costs of building its own capability to provide support to this large new group of users.

Governance Failure

Through a series of crises, a large government agency realized that it was incapable of keeping up with technology change. Leaders of the agency believed it could be much more effective in fulfilling its mission if its installed technology was much closer to "leading-edge" than "dinosaur." Outsourcing seemed the fastest way to resolve the problem. Agency executives determined that the service provider should also enforce standards across the whole of the agency's distributed computing operations in order to cut costs and improve service. After two years of evaluation and negotiation, the agency entered a contract with a large IT service provider. The deal was announced with great fanfare, and significant IT operations staff was transferred to the service provider.

Less than six months into the contract, problems became very apparent. The service provider was not receiving orders—and the agency had committed to minimum monthly payments to the service provider. It turns out that the different departments in the agency, while supportive of the original intention of using outsourcing to provide fresher technology, were adamantly opposed to having standards imposed. When the departments learned that they were limited in what equipment they could order, they found ways to place orders with other providers and avoided the contract altogether. The agency hadn't set up governance mechanisms to enforce compliance with the outsourcing contract. From there, the problems got worse—the agency was now incapable of providing support internally as its staff had been transferred to the service provider or moved to other positions in the agency. Less than a year into the contract, the agency began negotiations to completely restructure its agreement and started the arduous process of establishing a sourcing governance model to ensure that the new contract would be fully utilized.

Poor Coordination

The senior management of a global petrochemical company decided that the outsourcing of business and IT services should be part of its operations strategy. The executives mandated that the cost of any new investment initiative had to be compared to the cost of obtaining the required outcome via outsourcing. Management developed a rigorous business case methodology and implemented it across the company to ensure that outsourcing was considered before the company funded any initiative. For a long time, it seemed that the program was a roaring success. The company's annual spending on outsourcing was rising at triple digit rates—but not as fast as the estimated savings from performing the same services internally.

Three years into the program, the company launched a corporate audit and benchmarking effort to make sure that the savings figures were accurate and to assess the success of the program. The audit discovered that there were more than five hundred outsourcing contracts in the company and that on average the company was paying 20 percent more than market price for the services it was buying. The auditors discovered that, since the program did not require any central coordination of services contracts, there was no opportunity to leverage the company's considerable buying power. Additionally, the mandate on comparing internal costs to outsourcing did not require externally benchmarked pricing, but only required that the external providers be less costly than internal provision. As a result, although the company appeared to be saving money when it compared the outsourcing costs with internal costs, it was paying well above the market rates for services.

The Eight Myths of Outsourcing Today

Why is there now such a disconnect between theory and practice in outsourcing? You might wonder why problems are so prevalent when the recipe seems so straightforward: hire experts to provide the services that are not core or are nondifferentiating to the organization, and reap the benefits of improved management focus and more efficient and effective services.

The root of the problem, we believe, can be traced to eight myths that pervade current outsourcing management approaches:

1. *The myth of sourcing independence:* Sourcing is an element vital to the fulfillment of business strategy. But very often we encounter organizations whose sourcing decisions are made entirely independent of business strategy. The nature of outsourcing relationships formed is entirely incompatible with the business results expected. This often takes the form of dramatic disconnects between senior executives, the board, and operational managers.

2. *The myth of service autonomy:* A similar myth is that services are autonomous—and one sourcing relationship has nothing to do with another. This myth is a holdover from the days when only very discrete services (like food service and building maintenance) were outsourced. In today's world, service providers depend on each other and on internal services to meet goals—autonomous services don't exist.

3. *The myth of economies of scale:* Many organizations enter outsourcing relationships to cut costs. They believe that service providers' ability to leverage economies of scale is unlimited and allows the providers to offer services at a lower cost through "mass production." While this capability exists to a certain extent, the benefits of economies of scale depend on the service providers' ability to deliver standardized services to multiple organizations. In practice, though, many organizations want to enjoy the benefits of economies of scale but refuse to allow service providers to provide standardized services; the result is often disastrous.

4. *The myth of self-management:* Most organizations that enter outsourcing contracts do not have a coherent plan for the ongoing management of the relationship and the services that are provided. Consciously or unconsciously, they assume that the contract and the various service level agreements that are negotiated will be self-managing and that investing in governance processes over the contract's lifetime is unnecessary.

5. *The myth of the enemy:* Far too many organizations enter negotiations for long-term outsourcing contracts under the misconception that the service provider is the enemy. They view the contract negotiations as a war in which there will only be one winner. The usual result of this approach is that both the organization and the service provider end up casualties.

6. *The myth of procurement:* A related myth is that the sourcing of services is primarily a procurement exercise where best price wins. In reality, many services outsourced today are vital to

corporate strategy, and therefore issues of capability, culture, relationship, and other factors are often more important to long-term success than price.

7. *The myth of the steady state:* The most common outsourcing arrangements seen today envision a steady state—the outsourced services will never need to change. Nothing in business operations today remains in a steady state for long, and when the needs change, outsourcing relationships often break down.

8. *The myth of sourcing competency:* Finally, and perhaps most painfully, virtually every organization we deal with, even when accepting the need for ongoing common management across service providers, believes that it has the required management competencies in house to perform the necessary governance. Organizations learn too late that managing external services requires vastly different competencies than managing the same, internally provided services.

If you take a moment to review the preceding case studies, you'll see many elements of these myths and the destructive impact they have. Moving beyond outsourcing to Multisourcing requires dispelling these myths and taking a new approach to all sourcing initiatives and actions.

New Terrain Requires a New Map

MULTISOURCING is new terrain, different from our traditional approaches to outsourcing. While outsourcing unquestionably has provided substantial benefits, traditional approaches have become far less useful in meeting business goals, for all the reasons we've discussed. Multisourcing will deliver the promised business benefits that managers, executives, boards, and investors have expected from outsourcing. It will allow organizations to focus capital and resources on those items that really matter. It will allow firms to aggressively pursue growth opportunities while mitigating risk. It will allow greater agility, higher quality, and lower costs. Organizations must take a Multisourcing approach to compete on a global basis.

We strongly believe that the full value of blending multiple internal and external service providers can be realized, despite the challenges and despite the need for new approaches, because we have seen it in action. Organizations like Anglo-Platinum, DuPont, General Dynamics, Nike, Nextel, GE, Entergy, Tetra-Pak, Thomson, Sun Microsystems, Ontario Power Generation, and many others are beginning to apply the principles of Multisourcing and are moving beyond outsourcing to improve their growth prospects and their agility.

The problem with the current state of affairs is that while businesses, executives, and managers have wholeheartedly embraced the use of outsourcing, they are trying to implement and manage multisourced operations with the wrong approaches and models. The world of Multisourcing is new terrain for operations and as such requires a new map. This new map is needed to guide managers in the rational and effective management of a multisourced organization, one where internally and externally delivered services are blended seamlessly, managed and governed effectively, and evaluated continuously for effectiveness and efficiency. This book will provide such a map to Multisourcing's new terrain. The first three chapters are primarily about sourcing strategy, the vital foundation to effective Multisourcing. In chapter 4, we look at sourcing governance—your secret weapon for keeping your sourcing strategy on course. Chapters 5 and 6 examine how to select the right service providers and create the right contracts to enable success. Finally, chapter 7 looks at the ongoing functions of Multisourcing management and measurement—your tools to ensure that your changing needs are being met.

Four Key Themes

FOUR KEY THEMES are reflected throughout the book; they underlie and are woven through every aspect of Multisourcing. The book is roughly organized along these themes, but they are not sequential steps and each appears in every part of the book. You can consider these key themes a crash course in Multisourcing.

1. *You must have a strategy.* Considering the complexity of Multi-sourcing and the rapidly changing needs of today's businesses, an organization must have a comprehensive strategy for how it will use sourcing to meet its long-term goals. You will never achieve optimal performance without a well-planned and integrated sourcing strategy.

2. *Multisourcing governance is the single most important factor in determining success.* Despite the importance of strategy, governance is, surprisingly, even more important. The lack of a strategy will certainly be a huge barrier to your being fully successful, but good governance can help you achieve positive outcomes from your sourcing relationships and keep your Multisourcing environment from spinning out of control while a strategy is formed. No matter how good your strategy is, if you don't have sourcing governance in place to implement your strategy, enforce it, change it, and adjust it to market changes, your strategy will be worthless.

3. *Multisourcing is built on a network of relationships—not trans-actions.* Success via Multisourcing requires the understanding that you are entering ongoing relationships with service providers that will in large part become partners with you in delivering business outcomes. Managing relationships is vastly different from managing one-off transactions—it means that you have to be concerned not just about what happens today but about ensuring a positive environment for working with your service providers tomorrow. This approach needs to domi-nate your thinking in how you deal with service providers.

4. *Multisourcing requires creating measures that matter.* This may seem a truism, and we only wish it were so. Far too many service relationships founder, not because of a lack of measure-ment, but because of a lack of measurement of the things that

really matter. Service level agreements often measure inciden-
tal items that have no bearing on business outcomes. With
every step you take in Multisourcing, from strategy to governance to relationship management, you need to keep in mind
the imperative of creating meaningful measures that help
managers steer toward required business outcomes.

Who Should Read This Book and Who Shouldn't

WE'VE WRITTEN this book for executives and senior managers
who need help in shifting from compulsive (and often chaotic)
outsourcing to Multisourcing—executives who want and need to
improve cost structures, add capability, and expand globally, all while
increasing agility and creating competitive advantage. Because we are
writing for these executives who have a broad view of operations, we do
not delve into the vagaries or specifics of any particular type of service.

Our goal is for this book to be a guide to enterprise sourcing issues
for executive management, not a "sourcing for dummies" type of offering. Thus we have endeavored to keep the text readable and practical
without becoming too detailed. In general, you won't find step-by-step
guides, but you will see comprehensive discussions of the issues at
hand and proven approaches for achieving success. You will also see
some frameworks for decision making. These frameworks are intended
to stimulate internal discussions and to be used for examining various
approaches to your Multisourcing decisions. Our discussions are based
on years of working with thousands of companies helping solve outsourcing problems and create Multisourcing solutions.

We should briefly mention case studies. There are both named and
anonymous case studies throughout the book—all reflecting clients we
have worked with since 2000. In both types of case studies, we have
generally limited the details in these discussions for several reasons.
First, the details tend to distract from the main points; second, many of
our clients believe that their approaches to Multisourcing are providing

them vital competitive advantage in their markets today and want to preserve that advantage. Third, as we're sure you're fully aware, outsourcing is a highly politically charged topic currently and we do not wish to add further fuel to any fires. In the anonymous case studies, minor details of each story have been changed to protect confidentiality.

Finally, the book is the result of not just our experience but that of hundreds of our colleagues and the combined learning of our clients who live in the world of Multisourcing every day. We sincerely hope you will find what we've learned to be helpful in bringing order to the chaos and in moving beyond the challenges of outsourcing and to Multisourcing.

CHAPTER one

A Map to Multisourcing

Is YOUR ORGANIZATION A COMPULSIVE OUTSOURCER? Have you pursued outsourcing without integrated planning, strategy, and management? Like so many other enterprises, yours has almost certainly followed conventional wisdom and entered more and more outsourcing contracts over the last decade; you may not even know how many. Although some outsourcing initiatives have proven successful, in all likelihood you're finding that meeting expectations and achieving goals is becoming harder and harder. You're outsourcing more but finding more challenges rather than more solutions. In fact, if your organization is like most enterprises, your experience of outsourcing probably bears remarkable resemblance to the Spanish exploration and conquest of the New World nearly five hundred years ago.

In 1539, Francisco Coronado led a group of more than three hundred soldiers on a two-year expedition to find Cibola, better known as the seven lost cities of gold. Considering their experiences to that date, Coronado and his noble sponsors had more than enough reason to believe in the existence of cities made of gold. After all, they had seemingly reliable information and guides, and earlier expeditions led by Cortez and Pizarro seemed to guarantee success on a grand scale. Coronado proceeded to spend the next three years wandering across much of the present-day southwestern United States.[1] By the time he returned to his home base, he had lost half his men and apparently part of his mind when a horse stepped on and cracked his skull, but he had found absolutely no gold. Far from being celebrated as a hero for his work in crossing country that would not be traversed again by Europeans for three hundred years, Coronado was put on trial for incompetence.

According to Marc Reisner, author of *Cadillac Desert,* the greatest irony of Coronado's travels is that he must have ridden within miles of significant gold and silver deposits in Tubac and Tombstone, Arizona, without ever knowing they were there.[2]

Just as the early explorations by the Spaniards yielded fantastic results, spurring ever-grander expeditions and ever-more-outrageous expectations of success, so the last decade of outsourcing has generally been tremendously successful while generating increasingly irrational expectations. This is not because opportunity no longer exists, but because a new approach is needed to generate results. The same old approaches to outsourcing (such as service autonomy, treating providers as the enemy, and failing to invest in sourcing management competencies) will not generate positive business results today. If Coronado had mined for gold rather than wandering around looking for entire cities made from it, the entire history of the American Southwest would be vastly different. If you implement the disciplined approach of Multisourcing rather than relying on traditional approaches to outsourcing, you will be able to write a story of success rather than one of missed opportunity.

Why is this change occurring? One reason is that while outsourcing is not a new phenomenon, it is now pervasive. It has grown to encompass critical business services (such as finance and human resources functions, strategic IT deployments, and research and development) rather than just peripheral business functions (the cafeteria and mail room, for instance). Additionally, not only are more business services being outsourced, but these services must also interact with and rely on both internal operations and other outsourced services to an unprecedented level.

These changes signal an entry into new terrain for business operations—and therefore the need for new approaches. Without a map of this new terrain and experienced guides who can help put these new approaches into practice, organizations will have increasing difficulty achieving business success with outsourcing. This new terrain can be unforgiving for companies and for the executives charged with getting results.

The difference between Multisourcing and ad hoc outsourcing is that in Multisourcing, the enterprise consciously and proactively acknowledges, plans, and manages the interdependency of internal and external service providers. So, for example, you might outsource the administration of benefits and payroll. That service provider is dependent on IT infrastructure services provided by another service provider and perhaps a custom software application written and maintained by yet another service provider. Data needed for benefits and payroll is derived from a data warehouse maintained by an internal business intelligence center but managed by internal resources from the finance department. This complicated interaction of service providers, internal and external, is the de facto situation most organizations have arrived at via a decade of compulsive outsourcing. Using a blend of internal providers and several external providers is the new normal for business operations. Multisourcing, including new approaches to sourcing strategy, sourcing governance, sourcing management, service provider selection, and service measurement must be adopted to control and benefit from this new, but now normal state of affairs.

We've written this book because we've seen the ups and downs of ad hoc or compulsive outsourcing and the tremendous benefits when Multisourcing is implemented in a disciplined manner. Using that research and experience, we can help you create your own map and guide you on the journey toward Multisourcing. The goal of this book is not to hand you a generic map (which would be worthless, anyway), but to enable you to create your own customized map, specific to your organization. To that end, we will guide you in creating and implementing Multisourcing approaches in your organization.

Before we move on to helping you create your unique map of current sourcing operations, recall for a moment the definition of Multisourcing: the disciplined provisioning and blending of business and IT services from the optimal set of internal and external providers in the pursuit of business goals.

First, note that Multisourcing is not just a *better* way of doing outsourcing. Multisourcing describes how an organization achieves its goals by taking a long-term, holistic approach. Ad hoc, compulsive outsourcing leads to a tangled mess of disconnected deals that are poorly and redundantly managed and often ineffective in achieving the goals that really matter to executives. Multisourcing, on the other hand, recognizes a services value chain and the dependency of service providers on each other and applies consistent management across all services to achieve business outcomes.

A Guide to the Multisourcing Terrain

L IKE MANY EXECUTIVES who have plunged headlong into chronic and ad hoc outsourcing, Coronado was already significantly overcommitted before he discovered that the information he had about the seven cities of gold was unreliable. The failure of the expedition was compounded when, upon discovering that where he expected to find cities of gold, there were only poor villages, Coronado did not change his approach or tactics. He did not adjust to the situation, but began simply "trying harder" with his extant strategy. Most organizations unfortunately continue to follow Coronado's example and stumble blindly through their sourcing decisions believing that by trying harder—negotiating harder, writing tougher service level agreements, or replacing a service provider—they will achieve success.

Multisourcing requires a comprehensive and new approach—and that approach, encompassing everything from strategy to governance to provider selection, requires a thorough understanding of your present situation. It would be much easier if you had the luxury of starting from scratch, but you are probably already deeply committed to a large variety of outsourcing contracts. Before we can give you a guide to implementing Multisourcing, we have to explain what the landscape really looks like and help you find your exact current location.

To that end, in this chapter we present a series of frameworks for describing your services sourcing environment and the various relationships and deals that make it up. Think of these frameworks as a number of different perspectives on your sourcing situation or a series of progressively higher-resolution satellite photos of the terrain. We'll start at the broadest level, looking at the variety of sourcing actions (what you might think of as the satellite picture of an entire hemisphere); and then move to the various categories of services (the continent); and finally look at the types of contracts, deals, and the sourcing relationships (the country). Each of these views looks at your current sourcing situation from a different perspective so that you have the full view needed to begin planning a Multisourcing strategy. The situation is much like the old saw about the scientists in the darkened room trying to describe an elephant by only examining a small part. Without all these perspectives, you won't have the complete picture you need to plan your next steps.

Sourcing Actions

THE HIGHEST-LEVEL VIEW is, of course, the simplest. The work of every organization is the sum of a series of processes or services. Some of these services, such as payroll, accounts receivable and payable, purchasing, and customer service, are common, part of every organization. Others are highly industry specific or company specific. These include check processing in the retail banking industry, actuarial services in the insurance industry, drug testing in the pharmaceutical industry, inventory management in retail, and pricing and yield management in the consumer packaged-goods industry. All these services must be sourced from some provider. Multisourcing is the result of the increasing use of external providers for any of these services. There are four actions you can take for sourcing services:

Build (and maintain): Traditionally the default, this option means using your own people, infrastructure, and investment to build and deliver services.

Buy: With this option, an organization uses external sources for the provision of services. This describes traditional outsourcing, in which potentially any service may be bought rather than built. A variety of strategies for contracting exist, such as full-service outsourcing, prime vendor with subcontractors, and selective outsourcing, in which discrete components are purchased on a best-of-breed basis from multiple providers.

Cooperate: The third option is the acquisition of services through joint ventures, consortia, and models in which two or more organizations pool resources to deploy a solution, form a services company, or develop a shared service offering.

Compete: Finally, there is the option of putting an internally built service provider—your IT department or business process department—on a competitive footing by giving the group its own profit and loss statement (P&L) and the responsibility of delivering services to the organization or its subsidiaries on a fee-based or tariff model. This option is a complicated choice that straddles the line between build and buy. At its extreme, this model may also include spinning off the service provider as a branded service entity into the marketplace to take a service offering developed internally and sell it.

Every service your organization employs to function will fall into one of these four actions. The last decade of outsourcing growth means that, throughout your organization, you are almost certainly engaged in at least two of these actions to provide needed services, and these services are becoming increasingly interconnected. That is the nature of the new operational terrain. The first step to implementing Multisourcing is to recognize which sourcing action category each service in your organization falls into. You may have to get fairly granular here, as various elements of a service may involve different actions. For instance, although the human resources process or service may be built and maintained internally, the benefits-management service may be bought, while the hiring function falls into the compete category (the HR organization operates on a fee basis for managing candidate identification, interviewing, and salary negotiation).

Global Sourcing Options

T HE NEXT LEVEL of detail is to map where services are delivered from. The question of outsourcing and offshore sourcing is tremendously complex, not the least because of questions of perspective: Mexico will be *nearshore* to the United States and *offshore* to Spain. Furthermore, with global corporations who have presence and employees throughout the world, determining what is *nearshore* or *offshore* can become an academic debate. For instance, if Indian carriers of Citibank credit cards are routed to a call center in Canada, is customer service offshore? What if an organization's headquarters, service delivery personnel, and service consumers are all in different countries? A senior executive at a process manufacturing company that has been criticized for moving service jobs to India noted in an interview with us that if you compare the numbers of employees his company has in India with the company's revenues derived from India, then you would have to conclude that India is underserved in terms of jobs. "If anyone has a right to complain, it's the Indians. We've offshored jobs from India to the United States if you really look at the numbers!" noted the executive.

Partially because of this confusion of perspective, the terms *outsourcing* and *offshore* are often used interchangeably; *offshore* has also become synonymous with India and China. To complicate matters further, this erroneous conflation of terms has led to the creation of additional terms such as *nearshore,* to discriminate between the countries relatively near the service recipient and those on the other side of the world, and *farmshore,* to describe the placement of jobs in low-cost regions of the service recipient's home country.

We categorize service delivery location in relation to service consumers (which can be business units, departments of the organization, or customers) as either domestic or nondomestic (whether nearshore or offshore). However, this is not the full story. One also has to consider the ownership of the service delivery resources, not just their location. A nondomestic location does not necessarily mean the service is outsourced. Many large Western corporations (e.g., Oracle, Intel, GE, American Express, and Citicorp) have large internal operations in low-cost countries. There are four possible service delivery options in terms of location and source:[3]

- *In-house, domestic:* The services are internally built and maintained with personnel and resources in the same country as that of the service consumer.

- *In-house, nondomestic:* Also known as captive offshore, this option describes when an organization sets up its own operation in a different country from that of the service consumer. Includes nearshore as well as offshore sourcing.

- *Outsourced, domestic:* These services are bought from an external provider that delivers service, with personnel and resources in the same country as that of the service consumer.

- *Outsourced, nondomestic:* Services are bought from an external provider that delivers service, with personnel and resources in a different country from that of the service consumer; outsourced, nondomestic services may be nearshore or offshore.

While these categories are binary choices between in-house and outsourced, more and more often you see a blend of domestic and nondomestic resources being used to deliver services. We refer to this as a global delivery model—using personnel from all over the world to provide maximally efficient service delivery (particularly in terms of people costs). For simplicity's sake, we'll focus on where the primary service delivery work is being performed as the marker for which of the four categories a service best fits. The next step in creating your map is to categorize your set of services according to these four options.

Four Worlds of Sourcing: Service Value and Delivery

WITH THESE QUESTIONS of build-versus-buy and domestic-versus-nondomestic in mind, we can focus in on each of the services a little more closely, taking a different perspective as our satellite view zooms in. The next framework, which we call the four worlds of sourcing, considers the type of value received from each service and how it is delivered (figure 1-1).

Beginning with value measures, we can categorize any particular service by the nature of the value it delivers. The vertical axis shows the value of a service in terms of its direct impact on business goals. At the bottom are those services that provide operational outcomes. These are the services that other services and processes are built on. As such, their direct impact on business outcomes is hard to measure. For instance, imagine trying to answer the question "What is the value of your data network?" Therefore these services tend to be measured or denominated in terms of process or service metrics (e.g., bandwidth per dollar, trouble tickets resolved, or number of employees on a payroll). The focus of the management of these services over time is on increasing productivity, reliability, and performance, or lowering cost, or both.

FIGURE 1-1

The four worlds of sourcing

The four different worlds of service delivery are based on the type of value delivered and the amount of customization of a service. Each world requires a different business model for effective delivery.

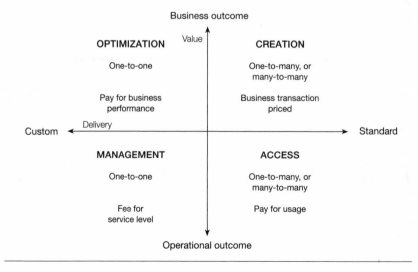

At the top end of the value axis is business outcome. These are services whose impact on business goals is much more direct and easily measurable in terms of, for instance, brand dominance, revenue enhancement, early-mover advantage, or competitive advantage. Rather than being measured in process efficiency, these services are evaluated by their impact on the business goals (e.g., customer satisfaction, market share, revenue, profitability).

To further categorize each service, we can overlay a horizontal axis that describes how the service is delivered. At one end of the axis are services that are completely customized to a specific organization's environment. Any in-house (build) service would fall at this end of the axis, but many outsourced (buy) services do as well. The service, while it may tap into standard processes and industry or cross-industry best practice, is adapted to the idiosyncrasies of the organization—its specific workflows, forms, customs, and culture. At the other extreme of the delivery axis is standardization, a one-to-many service in which the organization adapts itself to the way the service is delivered rather than the other way around. This delivery model is analogous to Henry Ford's famous statement about the Model T: "You can get it in any color you want, as long as it's black." The advantage of standardized services is leverage. The more recipients that use the standardized service, the greater the economies of scale and the lower the cost of the service.

We refer to this framework as the four *worlds* of sourcing because both providers' business models and recipients' value expectations are radically different in each. We should note here that many, many organizations' struggles with outsourced services are centered on the failure to understand and apply this concept in sourcing actions. Executives expect the cost benefits of standardization and economies of scale while demanding highly customized service. The result is, invariably, disappointment and strife between service recipient and service provider.

The *management* quadrant of the diagram describes a world in which the goals are predictable and often declining costs and operational efficiency and availability. Most outsourcing deals signed in the 1980s and 1990s fall into this world. When services in this quadrant are purchased from an outside provider, the financial model is based on a fee for a specific service level. The cost of the service rises if higher service levels (greater uptime, faster turnaround, etc.) are desired; the cost of service declines if lower service levels are acceptable. There is a one-to-one relationship between the enterprise and the service provider, be it internal or external. Services that might fall into this category include voice and data network management, data center operations, help desk services, and payroll. When these services are outsourced, the organization expects little change in the way services are delivered but expects to gain from the vendor's expertise and competence, and, over time, expects these leverage points to lead to lower costs.

The other sourcing world focused on operational outcomes, the lower right quadrant, is *access*. As in the management model, the value in an access model is an improvement in operational efficiency. Unlike the management model, the access model has the organization accessing a utility-like service, somewhat similar to the ways electricity and water are obtained. A company doesn't contract with the local utility to build a unique power plant at a nonstandard wattage, but taps into the power grid along with other customers. Thus it is a one-to-many, or many-to-many, delivery model. In practice today, we are only beginning to see the wide availability of access services, primarily provided by technology vendors. One instance of this type of service now common is the ability to rent bandwidth for limited periods to meet peak demand (think of an online retailer renting capacity in the lead-up to the Christmas holidays). The pricing model in the access world is typically similar to a rental contract. The organization pays for the capacity it uses.

In the upper two quadrants, the service model moves from an operational focus to a focus on business outcomes and business metrics. The top left quadrant, which we label *optimization*, is again a one-to-one delivery model, specific to the recipient's enterprise. In the optimization world, however, the recipient pays for specific performance levels that optimize the recipient's business model. As a result, payment schemes often depend on specific business outcomes, such as market-share growth, revenue growth, profitability, or entry into new markets, or are based on the service provider's earning a share of new profit or revenue generated. Because of the much larger shared-risk component of such relationships, they often also involve equity sharing. The use of a service provider by a major retailer to rapidly build an e-commerce site would be an example of a service in the optimization quadrant.

We call the final quadrant, the upper right of the matrix, *creation* because this approach to sourcing can create new revenue streams or new business value. Like its neighbor optimization, creation is focused on business impact or capability, but this model is delivered as a one-to-many or many-to-many relationship. Typical of the creation world is the emergence of new business models, referred to as business process or application utilities, for example, Salesforce.com. Salesforce.com provides customer relationship management software aimed at improving customer service and sales productivity via the Internet. The service recipient does not purchase licenses for the application or own the underlying technology infrastructure. Importantly, the recipient does not customize the software but adapts to Salesforce.com's configuration and process models. By forgoing ownership and customization of the application, the service recipient gains speed to implementation and greater control of costs, as the fees are based on usage. Covisint, the online automobile-supplier marketplace sponsored by General Motors, and other online marketplaces like it, would fall into this category as well because they create a many-to-many delivery model.

By categorizing the services your organization consumes according to this framework, you gain greater clarity on the current state of sourcing in your organization. You will undoubtedly see that not only are you using several sourcing choices (build, buy, cooperate, compete), but you are also employing services that provide different value levels and different delivery models. In categorizing your services, you've probably noticed that you employ many services that fall in the lower left corner of the quadrant and that may benefit from moving toward the lower right quadrant. We'll return to this discussion in chapter 3, where we introduce sourcing action plans.

Before we discuss strategies for better matching your services portfolio to your business needs, we need to have the satellite zoom in to another level for a different perspective. We need to look more closely at the types of relationships or deals that characterize each of your services.

Three Types of Sourcing Deals

WHEREAS THE FOUR WORLDS of sourcing look at the types of value delivered and the business models for effectively delivering this value, the final perspective considers the nature of sourcing relationships and the level of change expected from the service. Not all sourcing relationships are equal. Although often unspoken, the purposes and the expected outcomes of the deals vary widely, and therefore everything about them, from the selection of providers to ongoing management, should vary as well. Unfortunately, too many companies fail to appreciate this. We categorize sourcing deals under three broad types: efficiency, enhancement, and transformation.[4]

The first type—efficiency—focuses, unsurprisingly, on efficiency of operations, primarily in the form of cost reduction or cost control. These are the most prevalent type of sourcing engagements, focusing on delivering services at lower cost while maintaining quality and availability. An organization essentially taps into a provider's scale of operations to achieve cost reduction, gain access to technical capabilities, and offload the management of the service. The second type of deal— enhancement—optimizes a service or process to give an organization a tangible advantage or a new degree of functionality that did not previously exist. The third type of deal—transformation—directly affects the fulfillment of business strategy. Consequently, transformation involves a high level of risk for both parties and is generally formed as a partnership of equals between the recipient and the provider, with the goal of transforming the organization through a significant change in its business model and the creation of new revenues or improved profitability.

While we'll discuss these three types in much more detail, we should note up front that the categorization of a particular service-provision relationship is not permanent. Business expectations will change as outcomes are achieved. For instance, once an enhancement deal generates the improved performance sought, there will be an expectation of consolidating those improvements and lowering ongoing costs. Therefore, sourcing deals will optimally migrate between the three types over time (figure 1-2). Depending on the scope of a particular deal, different

FIGURE 1-2

The three types of service deals

The types of deals are related to the scope of change, the relationship complexity, and the business value expected from a service delivery relationship.

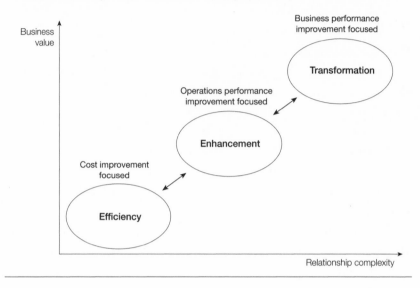

parts of it may fall into three different categories. Let's look at the three types of deals more closely.

Efficiency

Although they fit at the lower end of the spectrum of deal types, don't assume that efficiency deals are low value. These are foundation services; that is, they provide essential functions. An organization's goal when originally signing an efficiency deal was most likely cost control or cost reduction while maintaining consistency in service delivery. Additionally, the desire to offload management responsibility to enable greater organizational focus was probably a factor. The contract terms for efficiency deals should be heavily based on service level agreements that specify the quantity or quality of the service delivered. Efficiency deals typically include services that are commoditized, such as check processing, billing, mainframe operations, and desktop computing support.

Enhancement

Enhancement deals aspire to improve the current state of an IT service or business process. This may mean that a new IT solution is introduced or that a current process is reengineered. The goal is that, compared with the current state, significant enhancement will improve operational performance or outcome. While efficiency deals focus on controlling cost and improving reliability, enhancement deals typically focus on process improvement, often through innovation in IT or process reengineering. Contract terms should include measurement against operational outcomes, and the relationship between the service recipient and service provider becomes more important. The engagement requires that both parties have a clear understanding of the business goals to be attained and the business outcomes expected. As such, the relationship must allow for sharing knowledge of the recipient's business operations, for mutual understanding of strategy, and for processes to align the objectives of the two parties on an ongoing basis. This translates into greater levels of trust and comanagement with the service provider (which we'll discuss in chapter 4). Therefore it requires contract and governance models that will keep the deal current with changes in the business environment as well as reward the service provider for providing value beyond the original terms of the deal. Speed to enhancement is often critical, so lowest price should not be the overriding factor in signing these deals. Once the desired improvement is delivered and the new and improved service is stabilized, an enhancement deal is at a crossroads: it will either be managed in steady state with minor enhancements to ensure availability (not unlike an efficiency deal), or it must find new ways to enhance operational performance. Some examples of enhancement deals include developing and managing new enterprise resource planning systems, retooling and managing automated warehouses or shop floor operations, developing and managing improved

HR operations, and extending customer service into new hours, new locations, or new languages.

Transformation

A transformation deal is at the highest level of the sourcing relationship continuum in terms of business-strategy alignment. It also involves a closer partnership and therefore the most complex relationships between service provider and recipient. The goal in transformation deals is to innovate and dramatically improve the very competitiveness of the organization by creating new revenues, outmaneuvering the competition, and even changing the very basis on which a corporation operates. Transformational sourcing strikes at the heart of a company's business model.

Planning, implementing, and realizing the benefits of a transformational deal is an art form unto itself—the result of a high level of interaction, investment, and trust on the part of the organization and a provider. In transformational deals, critical domain and consultative skills are applied to a business problem or objective, and payment is contingent on outcome. Speed to transformation is critical, and the provider's ability to deliver the transformation and sustain it is the most critical factor in an organization's choice of provider. These are high-stakes games for both the service provider and the service recipient and often involve equity sharing or joint ventures. Some examples include developing and delivering a new product to market, creating delivery methods to enter new markets, and getting into a whole new line of business.

While at first glance it may appear that the three types of deals might be overlaid on the four worlds, this is actually not the case. Each framework represents a different perspective, a different aspect of service delivery and relationships. Efficiency deals generally fall in the lower half of the four-worlds framework, but they can encompass both highly customized and highly standardized delivery models. Similarly, both enhancement and transformation deals typically fall on the upper half of the four-worlds diagram, but would often overlap each other and again could encompass the entire range of customization versus standardization.

Draw Your Map

W ITH THE FOUR classification schemes discussed in this
chapter (sourcing actions, global sourcing options, four worlds
of sourcing, and the three types of sourcing deals), you can now realis-
tically draw your own map of your organization's current state. This is
the vital first step to achieving your business goals and moving beyond
simply outsourcing to Multisourcing. Before embarking on the journey
to Multisourcing, you have to know where you are now.

In table 1-1, we've created a sample map based on our work with
one of our clients. You may find this map useful as a guide in creating
your own map.

Let's look at a couple of the services to explain how we filled in this
services map. This organization has formed a joint venture to market its
finance and transaction-processing services to others; thus, the service
(labeled *finance* in the table for simplicity) falls in the *cooperate* category of sourcing actions. The joint venture uses both domestic and non-

TABLE 1-1

A services map

	Sourcing actions	Global sourcing options	Four worlds	Types of deals
Finance	Cooperate	In-house, domestic and captive, nondomestic	Optimization	Enhancement
Benefits	Buy	Outsource, domestic	Optimization	Efficiency
Payroll	Buy	Outsource, domestic	Management	Efficiency
Human resources	Compete	In-house, domestic	Optimization	Enhancement
Data network	Buy	Outsource, domestic	Management	Efficiency
Data center	Build	In-house, domestic	Management	Efficiency
Enterprise applications	Build	Captive, domestic	Optimization	Efficiency
Call center	Build	In-house, domestic and nondomestic	Optimization	Transformation

domestic personnel, but all are direct employees of the joint venture. For this reason, its global sourcing options can be described both as in-house, domestic and as captive, nondomestic. The service is delivered in a customized way for the recipient (the operation is based on the recipient's internal processes), with high business value, which puts it in the optimization world. Finally, the current aim of the service is to enhance operational performance (enhancement deal). Another key service, operation of the enterprise's data center, is maintained by internal personnel domestically. The operation is highly customized and focused on operational value measures. The goal for the service is efficiency.

Using table 1-1 as a template, you can fill out a similar matrix for each of your enterprise's core services. Doing so will give you a much firmer handle on the current state of sourcing in your organization and will serve to highlight some problem areas. But immediately trying to fix those problems is the wrong approach. You need to plot a specific course from your current state to where you need to be to achieve business goals, and it will require rethinking and retooling your entire approach to sourcing. Don't make the mistake of taking this map and immediately striking out in a new direction. Before beginning, you need to determine where you want to end up. Having a sourcing strategy is absolutely crucial to Multisourcing, and crafting that strategy is the topic of the next two chapters.

CHAPTER two

Prepare for a Well-Aligned Sourcing Strategy

EFFECTIVELY OPERATING AND THRIVING IN A MULTI-sourced environment requires much more than an executive fiat—your whole organization must adopt and internalize an evolved culture, new sets of processes, and new operating disciplines. Multisourcing is not a new discipline for procurement. It's much broader and deeper than that. It requires an entirely new way of thinking about how you function in a hypercompetitive, globalized world characterized by specialization; rapidly shifting partnerships, alliances, and competitors; and other rapid change. In short, to find your way beyond an environment of sourcing chaos, your organization needs a sourcing strategy, not just a few isolated changes. Thus, creating a sourcing strategy is where you must start your journey to Multisourcing.[1]

To illustrate the dangers of operating without a solid sourcing strategy that effectively links sourcing decisions to business strategy, consider these two real-life stories.

- A new chief operating officer (COO) was hired by a midsized European retailer. She had enjoyed a great deal of success in a similar-sized firm in a different industry, playing a vital role in streamlining operations and improving profitability dramatically. One of her first priorities was overhauling the retailer's human resources processes. At her prior position, she had realized major gains by outsourcing the entire HR function. After bringing in several vendors, she and her team spent a year and well over a million dollars selecting a vendor and negotiating a contract. As much as the effort was kept under wraps, word inevitably leaked out to the HR organization. By the time the contract was ready, most of the top talent in HR had left, finding jobs at other firms. But when the COO presented the plan and the contract to the board for final approval, she was met with incredulous stares. One board member, outraged, exclaimed, "Our people are one of our most valuable assets! What message would it send to our employees if we outsourced the human resources function? HR must remain an internal function." Although the deal was not consummated, the organization's HR performance suffered dramatically since the top performers had all left.

- The chief financial officer (CFO) of a multinational pharmaceutical company was becoming frustrated with the amount of time he spent managing accounts-payable and accounts-receivable processes built on out-of-date systems. He decided that outsourcing these business processes would reduce the drain on his time and his staff resources, encourage a better focus on the strategic needs of the company's business units, and allow for a complete refresh of the supporting technology without capital expense. The contract reached with a service provider called on the pharmaceutical company to pay a flat rate for the provision of accounts-payable and accounts-receivable services. The payment in the first year would not cover the service provider's costs for replacing the company's systems, but the gap would be closed in later years of the contract as the service provider's costs declined but the flat payment stayed the same.

    Two years into the contract, the CFO was shocked to receive a message from the company's CEO asking what the CFO planned to do to fix the horrible problems the company had with its accounts-receivable function. From the CFO's perspective, the deal was a huge success—costs were predictable, service had improved with the newer systems implemented, and the CFO no longer needed to spend any time dealing with accounts-receivable issues. The CEO, however, had just had lunch with a colleague from another company and learned that his colleague was paying far less for accounts-receivable services. The CFO eventually was forced out, the relationship collapsed, and the service provider was replaced at a huge expense to the company.

Stories like these are remarkably common today because so many organizations have rushed to outsourcing as a seemingly quick fix to a variety of problems—but even senior executives don't always agree on what the problems were. Successful Multisourcing requires creating a sourcing strategy that is closely, and continuously, linked to business strategy (see "Definitions of Business Strategy and Sourcing Strategy").

Because of the close connection between sourcing and business strategy, one of the primary reasons for outsourcing failures in organizations that have compulsively outsourced is the misalignment of sourcing decisions with business strategy. Such misalignment was one cause of the problems in both the aforementioned real-life examples, but the problems are more complicated than that. In both cases, there was also disagreement about the business strategy itself, even at the highest level of the organization. In the first example, the COO believed the business strategy was to drive as much cost as possible out of shared services, whereas the board believed the strategy was to contain costs within some shared services while improving the performance of others. In the second case, the CFO and CEO had radically different ideas of what a good deal was.

Causes of Misalignment

STRATEGY ALIGNMENT is practically a truism of business literature today. While it has been addressed by many authors in many ways, it is still a challenge for most organizations. We don't pretend to

DEFINITIONS OF BUSINESS STRATEGY
AND SOURCING STRATEGY

For clarity's sake, we should briefly define what we mean by business strategy and sourcing strategy before we discuss them further.

For our purposes, *business strategy* is the set of actions, programs, and other initiatives that an enterprise is currently undertaking to achieve its vision and objectives. These actions are determined in the context of, and must address, current business conditions, industry trends, the competitive and regulatory environment, and customer-value requirements. A business strategy defines what the organization will do, in what time frames the organization will do it, and how success will be measured.

A *sourcing strategy* is the set or portfolio of plans, directives, and decisions (what we call sourcing action plans) that define and integrate internally and externally provided services to fulfill an enterprise's business strategy. The challenge of a sourcing strategy is to continuously deliver to the organization the exact combination of internal and external resources and services that are necessary to support business objectives.

---

have the answers to all the questions of strategy alignment, but through our work with thousands of companies that have struggled to align their sourcing strategy and their business strategy, we have seen where the primary problems lie. We have found some solutions that have helped many organizations overcome the challenges of sourcing and business strategy alignment. We'll start by looking at the two primary causes of misalignment.

No Sourcing Strategy

The single most common cause of misalignment is the lack of an effort to align. Many organizations have no sourcing strategy at all, or if they do, they have not communicated it to operations managers. (This failing is not materially different from having no strategy.) In an important sense, the sourcing decisions made are random. In these organizations, sourcing decisions are taken on a one-off basis in a wide variety of locations around the organization, by many different individuals and groups. There are few, if any, guidelines to making sourcing decisions. Additionally, the organization typically makes sourcing choices only after making decisions on operations, technology, and services strategy. In this sequence of events, by the time sourcing issues are considered, the business strategy has been filtered through many individuals with many different points of view. The connection to the business strategy could most charitably be described as diffuse (figure 2-1). The result is not unlike the childhood game of telephone—by the time the message of business strategy reaches operations managers, it is completely garbled.

FIGURE 2-1

Sourcing strategy sequence

Typically, organizations execute sourcing decisions without an enterprise sourcing strategy. Sourcing strategy needs to be integrated with other strategy-setting processes.

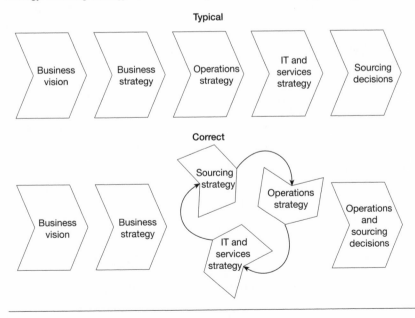

Not surprisingly, then, various executives could perceive any individual sourcing decision and its role in fulfilling the business strategy very differently—success from one perspective could easily look like failure from another. Most often, however, there is simply no connection between various sourcing decisions. Some are more closely aligned with the business strategy than others, but few are clearly tied to business goals.

The solution to this problem lies in reordering the sequence of strategy development and decisions. Choosing the right sources for required services is a fundamental question of business organization today and will only become more important over time—it demands a strategy rather than haphazard and random execution. Decisions about sourcing are only slightly less important than decisions about how the enterprise will compete in the marketplace, provide value to customers, and deliver returns to shareholders. The answers to all these core questions of business vision and strategy are built on how services and capabilities are sourced. Two organizations competing in the same market may have wildly different operations strategies, depending on how they choose to source the services and capabilities they require.

The development of sourcing strategy, then, needs to become co-equal with other parts of strategy planning, like operations strategy and IT strategy, rather than an afterthought. The proper sequence of strategy development (again see figure 2-1) requires that sourcing strategies be set as a direct outflow of business strategy. This sequence first of all helps improve alignment simply by proximity. Because the business strategy is not filtered through multiple and disparate lenses before anyone makes sourcing decisions, the ability to clearly align the highest level of sourcing decisions with the business strategy is much stronger. Making sourcing strategy a key part of the strategy planning process is an imperative first step toward Multisourcing.

Disconnected Business and Sourcing Strategies

Of course, a commitment to having a sourcing strategy and developing that strategy in close company with the business strategy doesn't guarantee alignment. (The question of governance—ensuring that specific sourcing decisions adhere to the stated sourcing strategy—is a different issue, one that we will address later.) Even for organizations that want to take a strategic approach to sourcing, the implications of a business strategy for sourcing are not always clear. Broad statements of corporate strategic intent, mission statements, and value propositions are valuable starting points, but are not enough—more detailed and actionable statements are needed. Compounding the problem is the all too common reality that the "real" business strategy isn't written down; it's in the heads and hearts of those responsible for implementing it. That's why it's critical to involve executive decision makers in developing a sourcing strategy.

What complicates the situation even more is that organizations tend to work on multiple strategic initiatives simultaneously across different organizational boundaries. Which initiatives in which business units take precedence or the level at which these initiatives should interact or be autonomous is not often clear. The decision-making process around sourcing initiatives and investments is often convoluted, and the range of possibilities unclear or presented in the wrong terms. When executives authorize expenditures for transitions from one source to another (be the transition internal to external, external to internal, or between various service providers), they may still not fully understand what they have consented to or what capabilities will be delivered to support their business.

Maxims: The Missing Link

IF YOU ARE TO CREATE a useful sourcing strategy, you must work with your colleagues on articulating an agreed-upon set of business guiding principles that clarify the implications of your organization's strategy—what we call maxims.[2] A *maxim* is simply a statement that specifies a practical course of conduct. The terminology used, of course, is unimportant. The critical piece is that maxims (or principles or guideposts or guardrails or any of a hundred other terms we've heard organizations use) must clearly provide direction; they must be commonly understood; and they must be actionable. Your sourcing maxims will act like a compass throughout your journey through the new terrain of Multisourcing. You can always look to them to make sure your sourcing strategy and sourcing decisions are headed in the right direction.

Business maxims express the focus of the business in actionable terms. They succinctly state what is most important to the enterprise. From business maxims, you can then develop sourcing maxims (as well as IT maxims, HR maxims, finance maxims, etc.). Sourcing maxims are statements that express how your enterprise needs to acquire and deploy services and capabilities across the organization to meet business goals and support the business maxims. Maxims, then, are the building blocks for the bridge between business strategy, sourcing strategy, and sourcing actions; they enable you to create shared expectations for the roles that internal and external sources will play in achieving your business goals.

Let's look in detail at the process of using maxims to create a well-aligned sourcing strategy.

Maxims Weave Together Business and Sourcing Strategies

The maxims process draws on the strategic context of the enterprise to tease out key business principles, and then works out what these mean for sourcing decisions (we'll use the term *maxims* from here on). Maxims create a very needed trail of evidence that weaves together business and sourcing strategies.

A maxim translates aspects of strategic context—strategic intent, business strategies, mission statements, customer value proposition—into terms that can be easily communicated and understood across the organization. These actionable statements then guide the creation of similar statements about sourcing that form the guidelines or guardrails to create a sourcing strategy. In essence, maxims serve as an aid connecting business strategy and sourcing strategy so that the goals of the enterprise are not lost in translation.

FIGURE 2-2

Connecting business strategy to sourcing strategy

Maxims fill the gap between business strategy and sourcing strategy and help ensure alignment.

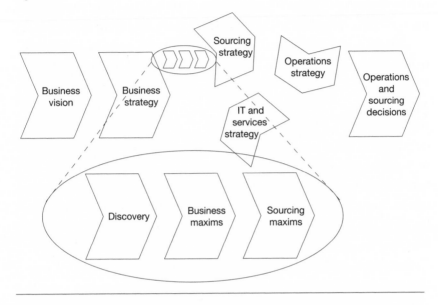

As shown in figure 2-2, business strategies are converted to business maxims, which lead to sourcing maxims and from there to the sourcing strategy. A similar process can effectively link business strategy to IT and operations strategies.

The difference between a maxim and a strategy is that a strategy states how an organization is going to compete in its chosen market. Maxims, on the other hand, state a shared understanding of what needs to happen in order to successfully execute the strategies. Maxims can focus the attention of all employees on key messages and do much to foster common understanding.

At first glance, using maxims may seem easy. However, the maxims process involves a great deal of work and attention. To be successful, the process must include three key ingredients:

- The participation of the enterprise's key leaders, who must agree on both the business maxims and the sourcing maxims

- General knowledge of the current state of the market for services required by the enterprise

- Deep knowledge of the enterprise's current strategies and initiatives, services, capabilities, sourcing relationships and contracts, core competencies, and management competencies

We'll work backward through this list, starting with the internal discovery process.

The First Step: Complete Internal Discovery Process

You'll begin the development of your sourcing strategy by looking internally to objectively gain self-knowledge about your current strategies and the actual state of your operations, costs, and capabilities. The goal is not to spend months and months collectively gazing at your organization's navel, but to have general answers to some fundamental business questions. In your discovery process, you will need to look at your enterprise's business strategy, initiatives, and competitive stance; human capital assets; knowledge capital; capability for managing change; organizational communications and politics; and risk tolerance.

Business Strategy, Initiatives, and Competitive Stance

For the purposes of supporting the maxim process, you'll need answers to questions like the following:

- What are our major goals for this fiscal year? What are they for the long-term planning horizon (whatever that horizon is in your organization)?

- Where are we in meeting our short-, medium-, and long-term business objectives?

- What are our primary ways of achieving differentiation, and are we gaining or losing ground to competitors in these areas?

- Are we able to respond quickly enough to unexpected changes in the business environment?

- To what extent do we want to benefit from synergies across business units, for instance, from common services like customer service, HR, finance, or IT?

- How important is the autonomy of individual business units or different geographies?

- What are our annual expenditures on shared services, and how do we expect these expenditures to change?

- Are current services and performance levels meeting the needs of the business?

- What is the organization's capability to absorb and manage changes?

Beyond these basic questions, however, you will also need to dig deeper into your current approach to sourcing services and capabilities. The work you did in creating your sourcing map in the last chapter is a huge step in the right direction. That map should define what services you are consuming and what capabilities you rely on, who provides them, the degree of customization and business value they provide, how those services are changing (or maintaining) your operations over time, and how these services and capabilities relate to each other.

Human Capital Assets

Turning a pragmatic eye on your existing staff and their skills is necessary if you want to answer the questions "What are we good at today? And what do we need to be good at tomorrow?" Many executives we speak with shy away from the idea of competency profiling, worried about the message it sends. This is an unavoidable step, however. Just as you would perform a physical capital inventory before making a decision about facilities, you must perform a human capital inventory before setting a sourcing strategy (see "Outsourcing and Attrition"). Without a common understanding of current competencies and which competencies are critical for future success, your sourcing actions will never be aligned with each other or with the business strategy and you won't be able to effectively integrate internal and multiple external providers of services.

This is also the time to consider whether you have built internal capabilities that may be more valuable to the market than they are to you. A global chemicals company (which we'll call ChemCo) faced this issue a number of years ago. After investing heavily in building a top-notch team to implement enterprise resource planning software across the enterprise, executives decided that the team they had created would be too expensive to maintain and would be more valuable to a service provider that could leverage the skills (and costs) of the team across many engagements. ChemCo decided that this highly prized and competent but expensive group was not core to its success and differentiation over time. The group was, in essence, "sold" to a service provider; ChemCo then engaged the service provider to finish the implementation of the software and manage the application over a multiyear period. ChemCo thereby retained access to this highly prized human capital without having to sustain the full ongoing cost of maintaining it.

Beyond an inventory of your human skill set, you need to get a grasp on the ability of your current staff in various departments to manage external resources if you choose to outsource. A far different set of skills is required for managing external providers than for managing internal ones. The difference is best expressed as a shift from managing *how* things are done to *managing the outcome* of the activity. Not all employees are suited to this hands-off style of management—if you are not already successfully managing external service providers, it is unlikely that you have the requisite skills in-house, or the skills may only be found in one department or business unit. Over time, most organizations will need to move aggressively away from technical competencies and toward relationship-management competencies (we'll discuss sourcing management competencies in chapter 4). As you focus on specific sourcing decisions, you'll need in-depth profiles of competencies and skills. At this stage you simply need a general grasp of the capabilities of groups across the organization. You need this information to ensure you don't create sourcing maxims that your personnel cannot implement.

Knowledge Capital

Just as you need to understand the state of your organization's human capital, you also need to know the state of your knowledge capital, spe-

OUTSOURCING AND ATTRITION

When deciding to create a sourcing strategy, which always includes the question of outsourcing, many organizations avoid assessing their human capital. They are afraid it will send a negative message to employees, who then may run for the exits. Attrition is a real concern and cannot be avoided—in fact, secrecy or avoiding evaluations of human capital will only make the problem worse.

In our experience working with thousands of companies in the sourcing strategy process, you should plan for a 5 to 10 percent increase over normal rates of attrition when you begin discussing the need for a sourcing strategy in a particular service area. However, if you attempt to hide your plans, dissemble with employees about your strategy and evaluation process, or create a climate in which rumor rather than fact prevails, you can expect your attrition rate to rise a further 40 to 50 percent.

The most important consideration, though, is not the attrition rate but *who* is leaving. In each service area, key personnel will be crucial to success in implementing and maintaining service delivery. You must identify and retain these people. Your best chance for achieving this is to be open and honest about the process and to engage key members of staff as early as possible.

Additionally, you must assess your human capital and thereby gain the knowledge necessary to be proactive. An assessment will help you identify which employees you most want to retain during the strategy and transition processes (if necessary) and may want to retain even after a decision to outsource. You also have to communicate early and often—a topic that we'll discuss later in this chapter and in the next few chapters as well.

cifically the state of information about the unique ways your organization operates and delivers value to customers. Some organizations have deployed Six Sigma or other methodologies across the organization and have very well documented processes and procedures. For other groups, this core knowledge resides in a variety of different systems, from data warehouses to intranets to HR manuals. At still other groups, most knowledge is undocumented and is floating around in key individuals' heads. Matt Arnold, a principal at Unimax, a manufacturing outsourcing consulting firm, talks about the importance of "tribal knowledge" when considering externally sourcing anything, from services to products. "In working with many organizations that are outsourcing production to offshore providers for the first time, I can't tell you how many times I've run into issues of the specifications for even the simplest bolt or assembly being wrong. When the customer rejects the prototype, there is often confusion—the product meets the spec. It always turns out that, for example, while the specification called for a part to be round, 'everyone' knows that it's really supposed to be oval. That's what I call tribal knowledge. It causes huge problems in manufacturing—and that effect is magnified when applied to processes and services that are not so easily measured objectively."[3] Before considering your business and sourcing maxims, you need to have general knowledge of whether your organization can explain and document requirements to external providers.

Organizational Communications and Politics

In preparing to formulate your organization's sourcing strategy, it is important to consider the politics of your enterprise and the implications of sourcing decisions on political issues as well as the quantitative measurement of your demands and costs. While outsourcing—specifically, using offshore service delivery—can be controversial, specific constituencies will have different reactions to your sourcing decisions, especially outsourcing, which carries a heavy load of emotional connotations of job loss, loss of control, and added risk. You must take into account and be sensitive to the internal political issues and cultural behaviors that swirl around outsourcing before creating your maxims.

To do so, you'll need to project how your organization will defend issues such as the transfer of staff, the loss of local jobs and revenues, and the loss of local tax revenues in the internal and external communities while you effectively communicate the benefits. Consider your appetite and that of other key executives and the board for dealing with the cultural issues and controversy that outsourcing can elicit in your employees, your shareholders, the press, and the public. Who in your organization will manage internal and external communications? Who will carry the torch for explaining and defending your sourcing actions? Are your executives prepared to digest and manage the different risks and the reduced control over how work is performed that outsourcing brings to their operations? Can your shareholders embrace outsourcing? And finally, how will your customers react to outsourcing?

As an example of what you need to consider, let's look at how three organizations handled outsourcing plans and the political implications. In the late 1990s, a U.S. state government was preparing to outsource its IT operations. The governor had specifically given the mandate to the state CIO to save taxpayers money by lowering the cost of IT operations through standardization and outsourcing. As the transition to an external service provider was begun, however, the service provider began notifying state employees about job relocations. None of the staff was being laid off, but the outsourcer was consolidating from several regional data centers to one central data center to control costs. These employees immediately went to the local press, which published screaming headlines about the state's "abandoning" local communities and capitulating to the bottom-line needs of an external service provider. The political fallout became so hot that the governor, who had specifically authorized the project with a noble goal—saving taxpayer money— had to order the project canceled. Because no one had communicated the benefits of the project to local communities—only to the state as a whole—when relocations came up, local communities turned rapidly and aggressively against the deal.

You may think that such a story is only relevant to government organizations—it's not. Every organization, public, nonprofit, or commercial, needs to consider the impacts of its sourcing strategy on local communities, the organization's sensitivity to the needs and opinions of local communities, and how it can communicate benefits to and influence local communities.

A financial services company we'll call Banking, Inc., is an example of a company that took issues of public perception seriously. The organization's mortgage unit was considering the offshore outsourcing of mortgage application processing but was extremely concerned about how the move would be perceived in the public eye. Banking, Inc., set up a program to allow mortgage applicants to choose, during their application process, where their information would be processed. Essentially, the customers could choose to have their application processed offshore, in which case they would receive a decision (positive or negative) via e-mail within twenty-four hours. Alternatively, they could have their application processed in the United States, in which case they would receive a phone call from a local loan officer within three days to complete the application. Over time, Banking, Inc., found that the vast majority of customers, when presented with the choice and the impact of the choice in terms of processing time, preferred the rapid turnaround of offshore processing. By putting the burden of the decision on the customer, Banking, Inc., was able to avoid any negative publicity around the decision to operate offshore.

You also need to consider internal issues such as how your workforce will react to outsourcing. Can you effectively communicate a sourcing strategy and its rationale without harming morale and witnessing a stampede for the exits? Consider your organization's capabilities for internal communication and how effective you have been at communicating strategy and changes in strategy. Also look at what mechanisms are in place to gauge internal reaction—most organizations are much better at understanding how the press perceives them than they are at understanding how their own employees feel. Another company in the financial services industry, IndyMac Bank, handled internal concerns about the organization's sourcing strategy, particularly offshore sourcing, head-on. At the very beginning of the evaluation of offshore services, the CEO hosted a companywide conference call to explain to all employees the strategy and the decision-making process regarding offshore sourcing and its impact on the current staff. The senior executives promised to the staff that offshore sourcing would only be directed at supporting growth, not replacing current staff; only natural attrition would occur—and the company has stuck to that commitment. According to Mark Nelson, executive vice president of Global Resources at IndyMac, communication was critical to alleviating staff concerns and keeping the company focused on growth: "Our culture is one of openness and straight dealing with all stakeholders, starting with our employees. The worst thing you can do is try to hide something, and leave people to speculate and create their own facts."[4]

In our experience, the best sourcing strategies are communicated often and from all levels within an organization—senior executives, management, peers of affected staff. Attempting to hide your plans or obscure the facts will create a climate of unrest and fear that you may never be able to heal. Evaluate the lines of communication between executives, business unit leaders, and staff before you create your maxims.

Risk Tolerance

Finally, within the internal discovery process, you will need to evaluate the organization's risk profile and tolerance. This evaluation requires not only an understanding of where your organization falls in broad categories of risk management, but also an understanding of how your organization perceives the risks of sourcing. For instance, some organizations consider the failure to engage outside partners far riskier than relying on outside parties. At other organizations, the use of outsourcers at all is considered highly risky. Of course, the amount of risk involved also depends on what you have already discovered in the aforementioned categories—if you have little experience with outsourcing, few of the competencies necessary for managing external partners, and poorly documented processes, then the risk of engaging an outside party is very high. Ultimately, you want to ensure that your business and sourcing maxims accurately reflect your organization's risk profile, perceptions, and experience.

Most sourcing-related risk falls into one of several major categories:

- *Transition risk:* the risk that during transition from one source to another, there will be major service interruptions

- *Service management risk:* the risk that you will be unable to effectively manage service delivery to provide the expected value

- *Financial risk:* the risk that the services will cost more than expected

- *Innovation risk:* the risk that innovation in service provision will not occur and costs or quality will be unacceptable over time

- *Business change risk:* the risk that the business needs will change dramatically and the services delivered will no longer be appropriate

- *Sourcing complexity risk:* the risk that the organization will be unable to integrate the variety of sources it uses and will thus incur breakdowns in service delivery

Note that none of these risks relates specifically to the provision of services by outside parties; the risks apply equally to insourced services. Judge how your organization perceives these potential hazards in relation to outsourcing and insourcing and the risk-management mechanisms you already have in place.

This process of discovery may seem overwhelming, but it is vital to the next steps in crafting a sourcing strategy. If your sourcing strategy is formed without this information, then you have little chance of successfully implementing it, even if it were appropriate for your organization (which it won't be!). This discovery step cannot be skipped or glossed over; the more detailed this evaluation is, the more reliable and effective your sourcing maxims ultimately will be.

The Second Step: Gather Executives to Articulate Your Business Maxims

With all this information on your internal situation and some basic knowledge of the services market, you are ready to create your business maxims. The maxims process brings together key enterprise and business unit executives—first to articulate business maxims and then to identify what capabilities are required for successful strategic initiatives. Usually at the heart of the maxims process is a structured executive workshop. These workshops are often not comfortable experiences for those involved; the sessions tend to foster heated debate about what really matters to the enterprise strategically. In fact, many executives may find the process threatening. Therefore we strongly recommend engaging external—and neutral—professional facilitators to assist in this step. We also find it helpful if the participants in such a workshop independently create their own list of business maxims and then share these suggestions with the group anonymously. This active but anonymous step helps ensure that all perspectives and issues are put on the table for discussion. The biggest danger in the maxim process is when the participants worry about being politically correct. They avoid saying things that may be controversial or uncomfortable (e.g., "We should outsource HR regardless of the cost because it doesn't make sense for us to spend time on that function") and therefore fail to surface the true sourcing issues that face the company.

The business maxims you create need to express several points:

- The firm's competitive stance in a clear, actionable way (or, in the government or not-for-profit sector, the mission and positioning of services)

- The extent to which the enterprise seeks to coordinate business units and to leverage synergies (e.g., autonomy of business units, cross-selling, and sharing of resources)

- The necessary capabilities and competencies to succeed

Using business maxims overcomes three common problems. First, few enterprises have the requisite sharp, comprehensive strategic statements; maxims provide the refinement and insight needed to reveal the implications of sourcing. Second, some firms have an excess of strategies, which are insufficiently focused and for which the implications are obscure or not readily actionable; maxims help narrow these down to an actionable few. Third, enterprise and business unit executives often do not collaborate on strategies; the *process* of executives working together on maxims is at least as important as the maxims they create.

Six Categories of Business Maxims

Business maxims can be grouped into six general categories (examples of maxims in each category are provided):

1. *Cost focus:* Price products and services at lowest cost; drive economies of scale through shared best practice

2. *Value differentiation as perceived by customers:* Meet client expectations for quality at reasonable cost; make the customer's product selection as easy as possible; provide all information needed to service any client from any service point

3. *Flexibility and agility:* Grow in cross-selling capabilities; develop new products and services rapidly; create capacity to manufacture in any location for a particular order

4. *Growth:* Expand aggressively into underdeveloped and emerging markets; carefully grow internationally to meet the needs of expanding customers; target growth through specific product and customer niches

5. *Human resources:* Create an environment that maximizes intellectual productivity; maintain a high level of professional and technical expertise; identify and facilitate the movement of talented people

6. *Management orientation and decision making:* Maximize independence in local operations with a minimum of mandates; make management decisions close to the line; create a management culture of information sharing (to maintain or generate new business)

It's possible to develop a long list of maxims, but we've found that five or six is the most that can be communicated by top management and absorbed by operational managers. Keep in mind that if you don't limit your maxims, you will most likely be unable to fund and deliver all the capabilities they imply. The important thing is that the maxims reflect the most critical issues and strategies at the enterprise level. Of these five or six, you must have at least one maxim that expresses the competencies necessary for success and one that specifies decision rights for strategies and initiatives (what level of autonomy do business units and geographies have?).

Now we turn to the next steps to move from business maxims to sourcing maxims. Sourcing maxims are needed to guide enterprise expectations for the role that internal and external sources will play in meeting enterprise goals.

The Third Step: Understand Your Sourcing Options

So that you can enter a conversation about sourcing maxims with a realistic, informed view of what is available from other sources, you need a firm grasp of the changing dynamics of the services sourcing industry.

Recall for a moment the four worlds of sourcing we discussed in chapter 1 (see figure 2-3 for a quick refresher). Traditional outsourcing, both in IT and in business processes, has been focused on the left side of the diagram. These services were highly customized and typically

FIGURE 2-3

Changing sourcing market dynamics

Providers have been progressively moving from the lower left corner to the right side of the four worlds to improve margins, the predictability of costs, and quality.

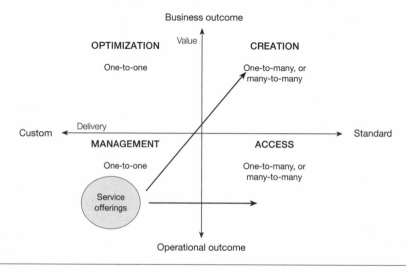

involved large asset and personnel transfers from the service recipient to the service provider. Recipients did not expect changed processes or service levels; they simply wanted lower and predictable costs, a way to avoid capital outlays, and improved management focus.

Over time, however, technology, market forces, and the needs of service recipients and of service providers have changed and therefore have forced the providers to adjust their approach. Technology, from high-bandwidth communications to the Internet, has enabled radically new ways of delivering services. From the recipient side, more and more organizations began looking to outsourcers not only for controlled costs but for dramatically lower costs or much higher levels of performance, or both. Service providers, on the other hand, have had to respond to the international capital markets that demand revenue growth and improved margins.

To respond to these forces, service providers have been moving aggressively during the past few years to create "in-the-box," easily repeatable, standardized solutions for their customers; other providers have focused on developing industry-specific best practices that are closely tied to business results rather than to operational efficiencies. Different service providers have succeeded to various degrees in making these transitions. Some services, such as payroll, mortgage processing, invoicing, and IT infrastructure, have moved quickly to standardized, operationally efficient offerings. Some industry sectors, such as retail banking, insurance claims management, and transportation, have more quickly adopted the use of outsourcing to improve business performance. As a result of these changes, many providers will no longer provide services that fall in the lower left corner of the diagram. In fact, some whole categories of services, IT infrastructure chief among them, are no longer available in a highly customized manner.

At this stage of the development of sourcing strategy, you need to familiarize yourself with the state of the market for the variety of services that your organization consumes. As a starting point, look back at your map of the services your organization is using. For each of the services identified, scan the market for what services are available, how they are delivered, and the level of maturity of the services. (The length of time these services have been offered and the number of users of these services is a good guide to maturity.) You can seek information at a number of places:

- Industry analysts and consultants

- Competitive intelligence on what services your competitors are using and from whom they are obtaining the services

- The major business press and industry journals

- Professional associations

Your goal is to gain not a deep understanding of the market for specific services, but simply a grasp of the state of maturity of each market and how services are being offered. This information will again help you create realistic and useful sourcing maxims.

The Fourth Step: Create Your Enterprise's Sourcing Maxims

Sourcing maxims are statements that express how your enterprise will acquire the skills, capabilities, and services it needs to achieve its goals, on the basis of the firm's strategic context, business maxims, and persistent business needs.

Here's an example of a sourcing maxim from a global manufacturing firm: *Common services will be sourced across the organization with an emphasis on industry best practices in order to control costs while maximizing effectiveness.* This might sound simple enough, but it has profound implications for how shared services are evaluated and sourced.

Because a major purpose of sourcing maxims is to explain the implications of business strategy and business maxims on sourcing decisions, sourcing maxims are best expressed as explanatory sentences. They need to communicate the *why* as well as the *what* of the maxim. Because one business maxim can have more than one sourcing implication, you will have more sourcing maxims than business maxims.

Examples of Translating Business Maxims to Sourcing Maxims

Let's look at how business and sourcing maxims can be used in practice to lay the foundations for sourcing strategy. Diversified Manufacturing, Inc., (a pseudonym) or DMI, is a multibusiness international manufacturing and services firm. One of DMI's business maxims is: *All operations are common and shared to create efficiency unless material improvement in results can be delivered.* From this business maxim, DMI developed the following as one of its sourcing maxims: *Individual business units may innovate and source services independently. Once cost savings or improved value is demonstrated, all business units will standardize on the new approach unless doing so will have a material negative effect on the business unit's bottom line.*

Some key words in this maxim are *demonstrated* and *material.* DMI didn't want to discourage innovation but also didn't want to forgo enterprisewide cost savings. These maxims made the CEO's vision about leveraging both local decision making and enterprise best practices actionable in terms of sourcing. DMI's service providers have been very happy with this stance as well—they know that if they can provide value to one business unit, they will have the opportunity to grow their business significantly. Because the service providers are motivated to innovate, all the business units benefit.

Based on our work in many organizations, table 2-1 presents some generic examples of sourcing maxims for each of the six maxim categories (obviously, not all would apply to the same firm). We've taken the business maxim examples described earlier and matched them with appropriate sourcing maxims.

As a reminder, keep in mind that your sourcing maxims *must* clarify three issues:

1. What competencies must be maintained or enhanced over time (one organization we worked with believes that sourcing management is the only competency that it must keep internal—all other competencies can be acquired from external service providers)

2. The organization's risk stance related to sourcing

TABLE 2-1

Converting business maxims to sourcing maxims

Various examples of business maxims and the sourcing maxims that might be created from them.

Maxim category	Business maxim	Sourcing maxim
Cost focus	Price products or services at the lowest cost.	To maintain market pricing leadership, always select sources that offer continuous improvement in operational efficiencies.
	Drive economies of scale through shared best practice.	Select service providers that drive standardization and mass customization to enable scale and economies of scale.
Value differentiation	Meet client expectations for quality at reasonable cost.	Services must be sourced from providers that meet client quality expectations at the lowest operational cost.
	Provide all information needed to serve any client from any service point.	Services that are involved with client information must meet enterprise standards for availability, security, integration, and distribution.
Flexibility and agility	Grow in cross-selling capabilities.	Internal sales and product-integration capabilities will be maintained at a high level.
	Develop new products and services rapidly.	Service providers must be able to scale quickly, be willing to adapt to changing requirements, and develop innovative delivery capabilities.
Growth	Expand aggressively into international emerging markets.	Service providers must be able to deliver scale quickly in target markets.
	Target growth through specific product and customer niches.	Service providers must deliver innovation and customization for specific growth targets.
Human resources	Retain professional and technical expertise differentiation over competitors.	Service providers must provide best-in-class professional and technical expertise and provide opportunities for internal knowledge transfer and knowledge management.
	Divest competencies that do not provide competitive differentiation.	All nondifferentiating services are externally sourced for best price to meet requirements.
	Identify and facilitate the movement of talented people.	Create opportunities for career development through both internal and external sources.
Management orientation	Maximize independence in local operations with a minimum of mandates.	Source for flexibility and adaptability to localized initiatives; local operations may opt out of enterprise sourcing decisions.
	Make management decisions close to the product line.	Sourcing decisions will be directed by line operations.

3. Decision rights for sourcing (a continuum between enterprise mandates, autonomous business units, and autonomous local geographies)

Remember the great advantage of developing maxims: when you finish defining your business and sourcing maxims, you should be able to link them all the way back to your enterprise's business strategies, long-term goals, and persistent business needs (see "The Interplay of Business Maxims, Sourcing Maxims, and IT Maxims").

Enterprise-Level Sourcing Governance: Keeping Things Aligned

As we noted before, there is a difference between having sourcing maxims that align well with the business vision and strategy, and ensuring that your sourcing decisions comply with these sourcing maxims. This process of compliance, of how decisions are made, who has input, and who has final say is a question of governance. There are several different areas of sourcing governance, which we'll address at various stages throughout the book. Here we briefly need to cover enterprise-level sourcing governance.

There are three parts of governance: elements, styles, and mechanisms. *Elements* are the categories of decisions that need to be made. *Styles* are about the participants in the decision, both those who have input and those who have a "vote" in the decision. *Mechanisms* are the ways a decision is reached (by a committee, an individual, a democracy, etc.).

Within the context of sourcing, there are three specific governance elements. Your next task in forming your sourcing strategy is to take your maxims and plan for the appropriate mechanisms and styles for each of these three elements of sourcing governance:

1. *Sourcing maxims:* Business vision and business strategy change, so your sourcing maxims will have to change as well.

THE INTERPLAY OF BUSINESS MAXIMS, SOURCING MAXIMS, AND IT MAXIMS

We've focused our discussion on business maxims and sourcing maxims, but there are, of course, other applications of the maxims process. In fact, the process was originally developed for use in aligning business and IT strategies.[a] One vital element in creating your sourcing maxims and ultimately your sourcing strategy is to examine the implications of your business maxims and sourcing maxims on your IT strategy.

Clearly, IT outsourcing has implications for IT itself, but many organizations fail to appreciate the dramatic impact of business process outsourcing on IT. Take, for example, a firm we'll call Food and Beverage, or F&B, whose IT strategy focused on standardizing its business applications on SAP enterprise resource planning software. SAP was used for finance, for manufacturing, and by the internal HR organization. F&B's CFO then decided to outsource HR—but the decision-making group did not include anyone from the IT organization. The selected provider used PeopleSoft HR software. F&B was then left holding the bag, having to spend hundreds of thousands of dollars integrating the disparate sets of data created by the two software packages on an ongoing basis.

This is a simple example, but it helps illustrate the core issues. Once you've created your business and sourcing maxims, you must consider your IT strategy (and, we hope, create some IT maxims) to ensure that they all align. No matter how carefully you work to align your sourcing strategy to your business strategy, if your IT strategy is not also in sync, you will inevitably fall short of your goals.

a. Broadbent and Kitzis describe how enterprises can make sure that their IT maxims and strategy are in line with their business strategy. There they explain the long-term goals for IT in successful organizations, delineate the five categories of IT maxims (roles, information and data, architecture and standards, communications, and assets), and give examples of useful IT maxims for each category. See Marianne Broadbent and Ellen S. Kitzis, *The New CIO Leader* (Boston: Harvard Business School Press, 2005), 90–97.

Some group (actual or virtual) must have responsibility for updating and maintaining the enterprise's sourcing maxims.

2. *Sourcing initiatives:* This element is not about specific choices, but about defining who has the authority to make choices related to sourcing. You can think of it as the authority to enforce the enterprise's sourcing maxims. What group or individual will ensure that the sourcing choices and deals made throughout the enterprise conform to the maxims?

3. *Sourcing management:* This is the ongoing piece of sourcing governance. Who will select service providers, manage service delivery and coordination on a day-to-day basis, and evaluate providers? Who will reconcile risk and business outcomes?

The maxims process isn't a onetime event. Your maxims need to be maintained and updated over time as your business vision, strategy, and circumstances change. Every organization needs a group of executives who will, at least annually, review the sourcing maxims to determine if changes are needed. Most organizations we work with create a sourcing council made up of executives from common services (IT, HR, and finance), if any, and from each of the business units. The sourcing council becomes the highest level of authority for sourcing-related issues throughout the organization. It is imperative that the members of the sourcing council have intimate knowledge of both the current state and the future plans of their area, but they also must have the authority to enforce the council's decisions in their area. DuPont, for instance, has an HR sourcing council that is made up of senior executives from every business unit as well as the CIO.

The sourcing council will also have responsibility for deciding who will oversee the other sourcing governance elements (we'll discuss these other elements in detail in chapters 4 and 7). Some organizations, like Thomson, Sun Microsystems, and American Express, have appointed an executive-level chief sourcing officer (see "Chief Sourcing Officers"). Some have given this oversight role to an existing executive—the COO or the CFO. Other organizations, whose business strategy dictates more autonomous business units, create a sourcing committee for each

CHIEF SOURCING OFFICERS

The chief sourcing officer is a relatively new executive-level position that a number of large organizations have implemented to bring oversight to sourcing actions and decisions across the enterprise. There is no template for the roles and responsibilities of a chief sourcing officer, and every organization that creates the position uses a different approach. Grant Reusch, chief sourcing officer at Sun Microsystems, was appointed by CEO Scott McNealy in 2004. "Scott and the board decided that we needed much more focus in all of our sourcing decisions, from components to business process services, to enable us to be more competitive," says Reusch.[a] Reusch and his team are responsible for overseeing every sourcing decision the company makes.

Barbara Scarcella, strategic sourcing officer at Thomson, was formerly the CIO of one of the organization's many divisions. "My staff and I had been very successful at bringing order to IT sourcing decisions in our division, reducing costs, and improving service levels at the same time," notes Scarcella. When Thomson moved from being a holding company to being an operating company, Richard Harrington, Thomson's CEO, asked Scarcella to begin looking at ways the enterprise could benefit from more central control of IT sourcing, as well as other common services. Today Scarcella and her team work as coaches and guides in sourcing decisions throughout Thomson, overseeing more than US$1 billion in annual spending.[b]

a. Grant Reusch, chief sourcing officer, Sun Microsystems, telephone interview with authors, September 17, 2004.
b. Barbara Scarcella, chief sourcing officer, Thomson, telephone interview with authors, January 4, 2005.

business unit, which then is overseen by the enterprise sourcing council. In other organizations, the sourcing council creates decision templates or a set of rules that must be followed; sourcing decisions can be made throughout the organization but must follow the rules and are subject to audit by the sourcing council.

If you've followed the advice so far, your sourcing maxims will provide some guidance here, as your maxims should define where the decision rights for sourcing decisions should reside. There is no right answer to what mechanism should be used to oversee the sourcing initiatives area—the choice depends on the individual organization's business strategy and enterprise governance approach. Whatever the approach is, however, be it a chief sourcing officer, a sourcing committee, or another alternative, it must enforce compliance with the sourcing maxims.

The final sourcing governance element is sourcing management. Since management is the largest and most continuous aspect of sourcing governance, we'll devote a whole chapter to it later in the book. Here it will suffice to say that part of your work is to recognize and plan for a mechanism that will have authority over sourcing management.

Building Your Sourcing Strategy

W ITH YOUR SOURCING MAXIMS defined and enterprise governance plan set up for sourcing decisions, you are now ready to create your sourcing strategy—the sum of all the sourcing plans the sourcing committees will create. How to create these plans, which must be specific to each service and capability your organization needs, is the focus of the next chapter.

three

Build Your
Sourcing Strategy

Your enterprise's sourcing strategy is the sum of your planned actions for each service needed for the achievement of business goals. It is a portfolio of sourcing action plans that specifically show where you are today and where you need to be over a defined period in the provision of your services—what services will be provided internally, which externally, where they will be provided from, and what amount of change in those services is required. Multisourcing requires that you apply the same rigor to all your sourcing decisions; none of them should be made ad hoc. As a result, your organization will need to make decisions about many of your services in parallel. This is why we stressed developing enterprise-level sourcing governance in the last chapter. Everyone in the enterprise must understand and agree to the ground rules for sourcing as exemplified in your sourcing maxims; there also has to be a mechanism for making and enforcing sourcing choices.

The structure of a book is linear, however, and not parallel. Therefore, in this chapter, we will present in a linear fashion the necessary steps for developing a sourcing action plan for each of your services.

Note, however, that you will be following these steps many times over, and often in a cyclical fashion (which we'll discuss later). Taking these steps for each of your critical services will create a portfolio of sourcing action plans—your sourcing strategy—that will lead you to Multisourcing and the ability to use sourcing strategically for achieving business goals. When you've finished this process, you can update your map from chapter 1 to show not only where you are today, but also where you want to be tomorrow.

The Five Key Questions for Building Your Sourcing Action Plans

THE QUESTION we hear most often from clients regarding sourcing strategy could be paraphrased, "Should I outsource or not?" The second most common is, "The board/CEO/other party says we have to outsource; what should we do now?" Both are symptoms of compulsive outsourcing. Unfortunately, in the vast majority of cases, these are the wrong questions. Or put another way, there are critical questions that have to be asked and answered first. Building a sourcing strategy, within the guidelines of your sourcing maxims, is not simply a question of "in or out?" Building your sourcing strategy requires carefully considering each service your organization consumes today or will need tomorrow and asking the right questions in the right order (an order slightly different from what we considered many of these same issues in chapter 1) for each service.

Your sourcing maxims set the guidelines, and the sourcing council or another executive group determines who will answer these questions. To create your sourcing action plans and build your sourcing strategy, you'll need to evaluate each of the services you identified in chapter 1, and consider five questions in order:

1. What are the business outcomes expected of this service?

2. How should the service be delivered for maximum value?

3. Where should this service be performed?

4. Should this service be retained internally or outsourced?

5. Will my service choices generate the needed return on investment?

This series of questions, although presented linearly, is ultimately cyclical. The answers you give at various stages may require you to return to the beginning and reconsider your earlier answers. And, of course, asking these questions will become part of your yearly strategic planning processes, for the answers will almost certainly change year to year as the market and competitive environment evolve.[1]

Question 1: What Are the Business Outcomes Expected of This Service?

A T THE ROOT of innumerable failed outsourcing relationships is a misplaced focus by organizations—right from the very start. These organizations overspecify their service needs in the initial phase of the process, and everything goes downhill from there. This may seem an odd statement to make—many clients we speak with presume that their struggles are based on *underspecifying* their needs, and that service deficiencies result from leaving too many details fuzzy. In some sense, they are correct; they have underspecified the outcomes they expect, while overspecifying how those outcomes will be achieved.

Most outsourcing relationships today have been built on a tradition of suspicion and the fear of loss of control—the myth of the enemy we discussed earlier. Recipients have perversely entered into highly dependent relationships with service providers, all the while believing that the provider cannot be trusted. To alleviate these fears of loss of control and untrustworthiness, the service recipients have typically focused their attention on ensuring that the service providers performed the assigned tasks exactly as the services had been performed internally, believing that this would protect the recipients' interests.

Traditional services outsourcing contracts have been built not around outcomes but around inputs. To clarify, consider how manufacturing outsourcing is typically denominated: around deliverables or outcomes. When a manufacturing company outsources production of a widget, it specifies the shape, size, and number of widgets it needs in what time frame. Or when a clothing company sources shirts from an offshore provider, it specifies the dimensions, material, color, and number of shirts it wants. Imagine, however, if the manufacturing company wrote its contract around how many lathes, lathe operators, and kilowatt-hours the outsourcer used. Or imagine if the clothing company specified the horsepower rating of the motors of the textile factory's sewing machines and exactly which people, by name, would do the sewing. At a casual first glance, we would reject these latter approaches as silly and counter-productive. Nevertheless, this is how most companies, even today, contract for services.

They do not specify an outcome (business or operational metrics); they specify how the work should be done (number of personnel, process diagrams, etc.). In short, they have not focused on *what* work needed to be performed but on exactly *how* the work would be performed.

Why is this a problem? Because it is self-defeating to the typical enterprise's goals in outsourcing—lowering cost and improving service performance. As Francisco D'Souza, COO of Cognizant Technology Solutions, an IT service provider, notes, "When a client specifies how work has to be done, it reduces our ability to bring our best practices to bear. If a client lets us determine the best way to do the work for them, that's when we can add the most value. Outcome-based [relationships] allow for a win-win situation between a client and their outsourcing partner."[2] When the service recipient specifies how work is to be done, this arrangement dramatically limits the service provider's ability to provide cost savings through efficiency (which cannot be applied, because of the highly customized nature of the "how"). Nor can the provider deliver improved service through process expertise (which cannot be applied, because it would require a change in the "how").

The net result is that the service provider's goals and the recipient's goals end up in direct conflict. While the provider wants increased revenue and higher margins, the recipient wants lower costs and better service; with the work highly specified, there is no way to resolve this conflict favorably for both parties. Typically in these situations, the service provider will move its best, most expensive personnel off the project and move in lower-cost resources: the A-Team is replaced by the F-Troop. This approach meets the provider's needs for adequate margins on the deal, but service invariably degrades for the recipient. The recipient's typical reaction is then to try to add even more specifications so as to improve service or to enforce penalties to drive service costs down. What quickly ensues is a downward spiral that sucks both recipient and seller into a black hole. No wonder so many sourcing relationships fail to meet expectations!

There are additional issues. When a service recipient closely specifies how work is done, there is a need for a great deal of oversight for ensuring compliance. For service recipients, this means retaining more and more employees to look over the shoulder of the providers to make sure they are following the enterprise directives to the letter. We once worked with a client that had eighty employees monitoring the work of forty outsourced personnel. While this may sound ludicrous (and it is), it is remarkably more common than most would expect.

So what is the way out of this dilemma? When forming your sourcing action plans, you need to focus on defining the outcomes needed from services, not how those outcomes will be achieved. More specifically, the more you focus on defining outcomes in business terms (cost savings, time to market, calls answered, applications or claims processed, increased revenue, etc.), the greater your chances for success in Multisourcing. Of course, not all services can be quantified in business terms, because their impact on business value is unclear. This is typically the case for infrastructure services like distributed computing, networking, and payroll. Even in these cases, however, the expected outcomes, rather than processes, must be defined.

Make no mistake, defining services in terms of outcomes is not an easy task. Operations managers typically have spent their whole careers becoming experts in how services are performed and how processes work and tweaking them for incremental benefit. They are not used to looking at services solely as outcomes—and often are afraid of relinquishing a large measure of the control they have typically exerted. This is not solely the fault of service recipients. Service providers have often been equally reluctant to commit to outcomes without limiting their risk by specifying exactly how much resources they will have to devote to achieve the outcomes. Success in Multisourcing requires moving beyond this faulty construct of traditional outsourcing relationships (although we should note that the preceding description could also apply to internal service delivery relationships at many organizations).

Outcome-based specifications require trust between the service provider and the service recipient—trust that typically exists when services are provided in-house but that does not extend to service providers. Before you let a fear of the loss of control guide you into over-specifying, consider this: why would you enter a relationship with an external service provider that you don't believe you can trust? If you are willing to source a service from outside, then you must build trust relationships with the providers. In Multisourcing, trust is a critical issue that we'll return to later.

Don't misunderstand. We are not advocating that you turn a blind eye to how services are performed; doing so is also a recipe for disaster. Auditing and inspection are a necessary part of risk management in sourcing, and you will need to ensure that your service provider, internal or external, is following certain rules. Oversight is especially necessary in the regulatory environment ushered in by the Health Insurance Portability and Accountability Act (HIPAA) and the Sarbanes-Oxley legislation in the United States and the Basel II financial regulations and privacy regulations in Europe (and of course, similar regulations rapidly being put in place around the world). Nevertheless, as you are developing your sourcing strategy, you must be open to a variety of solutions to your business challenges, not just the solutions that you already know and understand. Multisourcing will never achieve outcomes like improved agility and growth if the recipient controls how work is done. Thus, your focus has to be on outcomes.

Here are some examples of service outcome statements for a variety of services:

- *Payroll:* Pay all employees in the United States, Canada, and the United Kingdom accurately, following all applicable reporting and tax regulations.

- *Recruiting:* Provide three qualified interview candidates for each opening.

- *Accounts payable:* Process invoices within seventy-two hours of receipt.

- *Network management:* Provide adequate bandwidth to all locations, with no significant downtime.

- *Distributed computing:* Provide end-to-end uptime (PC, applications, network connectivity) to all users.

- *Help desk:* Resolve user problems expediently and with high-quality customer service.

- *Customer service:* Answer customer calls quickly, and raise levels of customer satisfaction.

Note that the outcome statements need not be highly specific at this point, although details won't hurt. You will define exact measures and metrics when you convert these outcome statements to service level agreements during the provider evaluation and selection processes.

As you are specifying outcomes, you need to make sure you are looking at both near-term and long-term needs. Consider how the need for this service will change over the course of the planning horizon your organization uses, be it two, three, five, or ten years. Are the outcomes becoming harder or easier to achieve? Is the service becoming more or less critical to business needs? Returning to the preceding outcome-statement examples, you will want to specify, for instance, that you plan to have employees in three additional countries in two years or you expect customer call volume to double within three years.

You'll use this combination of information—what outcomes are needed and how those needs are changing—to determine the type of deal you need for the service in question. In chapter 1, we discussed the three types of service deals: efficiency, enhancement, and transformation. Efficiency services focus on cost control and are appropriate when business outcomes can be very specifically and objectively measured, and where the quality of business outcomes is not expected to change significantly (the "amount" of service may change up or down, however). In specifying efficiency services, your outcomes may include specific cost reductions over time, such as in this stated outcome: *maintain adequate uptime for end users, while reducing cost per user by 10 percent per year over three years.* Enhancement services are focused on improving productivity and are needed when the quality (rather than the amount) of outcome is expected to increase substantially. Transformation services focus on creating new competitive advantages and market differentiation.

Because the difference between contracts, management approaches, and (often unspoken) business outcomes expected can be very large, it is important that outcomes match the deal types when you begin developing your sourcing strategy. As an illustration, consider Entergy, a large U.S. public utility headquartered in New Orleans. The company approached us in 2001 for help in determining how its current outsourcing relationship could be improved. A series of interviews, workshops with both Entergy and its service provider, and benchmarks showed that there were significant problems in the relationship because of a mismatch between the contract signed by the parties and both parties' expectations of the deal. While the relationship was still healthy at that point, many minor issues just below the surface would have eventually caused a major disruption. Essentially, both Entergy and the service provider expected innovation and operational improvement from the deal—what we would call an enhancement deal. But the contract had only really encouraged efficiency services. As a result, the client began to feel that service costs were too high (or the value delivered was too low). Meanwhile, the service provider believed that Entergy's close oversight of service levels that were focused on efficiency impeded any innovation on the provider's part. By slightly restructuring the contract so that it matched expectations, improving communications, and adjusting Entergy's relationship and service-management approaches, both parties were able to put the deal back on the right path. Rather than shrinking, as the client expected when it engaged us, the deal actually grew over the next several years.

Note that specifying the business outcomes and the type of service deal does not indicate in any way whether the service should be provided internally or externally. The service provider that leads a transformation to provide business outcomes could very well be inside the organization.

There is another important aspect of delineating the expected outcomes—it determines the scope of services to be aggregated for evaluation purposes. Group services together as long as they have a similar class of expected outcome. For instance, the category of HR services includes numerous subprocesses or subservices: payroll, recruiting, benefits management, competency testing and inventory, training, performance management, and so forth. The decision on how to break up or aggregate services should be based on the types of outcomes required. Some organizations view all of HR from the perspective of efficiency. Others expect efficiency from payroll, enhancement from recruiting, and transformation from benefits management. Grouping together services with different expected outcomes will limit your ability to effectively manage your multisourced environment. Group services with similar outcomes; disaggregate services with different outcomes and evaluate them separately.

At this stage, take the services map you created at the end of chapter 1, and update it to show the decisions made for each service. Some of the original services listed may need to be split into different categories; others may be combined. Your map should show the appropriate type of deal for each service and identify the expected business outcomes. At the end of this chapter, we've updated our sample map from chapter 1 to show these changes.

Once you've identified the business outcomes necessary and the level of change and investment (if any) required for those outcomes, you need to consider how your services will be delivered. This is not a question of who delivers the services, but a question of the type of value and the uniqueness of service delivery regardless of who performs the service.

Question 2: How Should the Service Be Delivered for Maximum Value?

W E HAVE ALREADY introduced the four worlds of sourcing. Your next step in building your sourcing strategy is to return to that diagram, now considering not where your services fit within it today but where they need to be for organizational success. Here we define success broadly, that is, not just reaching your goals but reaching them in the most efficient and sustainable manner.

Briefly, let's review the four quadrants of the diagram (figure 3-1). The horizontal axis measures how customized or unique the service or process is to your organization (most internally delivered services will be highly customized). On the left side are enterprise-specific services, and on the right are standardized services designed for mass delivery. The vertical axis considers the type of value the service delivers. At the top are value measures that relate directly to business goals as they are communicated to, and understood by, shareholders: top-line growth (revenue), bottom-line growth (profit), return on invested capital, and reputation. Toward the bottom are value measures focused on operations, whose connection to business outcomes may be harder to measure.

In the first step of developing an action plan for a service, you defined the business outcomes required. These outcomes will not only determine the appropriate deal type for each service but also point out where a service falls on the vertical axis. For example, earlier in this chapter, we looked at the following business outcome statement for customer service: *answer customer calls quickly, and raise levels of customer satisfaction.* Customer satisfaction can be tied to revenue (depending, of course, on how well understood the organization's business model is). Such a service would fall higher on the value axis than the expected-outcome statement for network management: *provide adequate bandwidth to all locations, with no significant downtime.*

Deciding where a service should sit on the horizontal axis can be a good bit trickier. Remember that here we are not describing the service as it is delivered today but how the service *should* be delivered tomorrow. There are three aspects to consider:

FIGURE 3-1

Choosing among the four worlds of sourcing

Organizations need to consider the interplay of outcomes and customization in service delivery. Business models for delivering services change, depending on which quadrant they occupy.

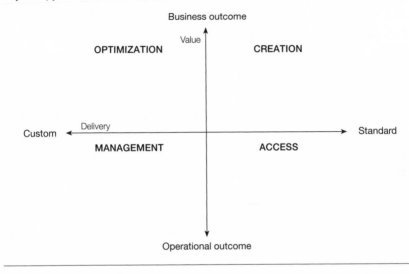

1. *Cost:* Plain and simple, customization is expensive. "Have it your way," may be the familiar slogan of one leading fast-food chain, but in the sourcing world, having it your way means paying a premium price. The relative cost of a service almost entirely depends on scale; the more that scale economies can be realized, the less a service costs. Highly customized services cannot be leveraged and therefore are relatively expensive. While cost efficiency or even cost improvement is a valid expectation in an organization's sourcing decisions, the expectation of volume pricing for customized services is unrealistic— commodity pricing is only available for standardized services.

2. *Governance and change management:* Governance and change management lie at the heart of whether you can access scale even if you want to. Standardized services often sound great

from a cost perspective, but standardization may not be easy to achieve, even when using internal delivery (see "The Private-Utility Option"). Consider whether all your business units use the same processes for similar work. In most cases, the answer will be no. Recall from the introduction the example of the government agency that tried to use outsourcing to enforce standardization. The organization, in essence, assumed that outsourcing would fix its inability to enforce standardization internally. This is a common assumption and is always wrong. Before you decide that standardized services are the right way to go, you need to evaluate whether everyone in your organization will either willingly accept, or can be forced to accept, a standardized service. This is where many service delivery models break down. An organization wants standardized costs and assumes it will be able to accept standardized services, but over time, it tries to customize the service delivery. In such situations, bad outcomes are inevitable—either cost savings will not be realized, quality will suffer, or the service provider (internal or external) will fall under tremendous cost pressure. Consider whether you can enforce standardization and whether your organization is capable of changing the ways it operates to accept standardized services.

3. *Integration:* A third consideration is the degree to which the service in question must integrate with other customized or unique services. Remember that you are living in a Multisourced environment. Again, the cost profile of standardized services is inevitably appealing, but the cost implications may not all be immediately apparent. While you may be willing to change to a standardized HR service and, through governance, to enforce adoption, you also have to consider how many other processes and service providers, internal and external, integrate with your HR processes. Will all these processes, most likely customized, need to be changed to integrate with the new way of doing HR?

THE PRIVATE-UTILITY OPTION

We speak to a number of organizations that are considering creating a *private utility,* that is, a customized infrastructure-provision service (for IT, HR, finance, or another service) at low cost. They believe they are large enough to create economies of scale within their own operation, without needing to access a standardized, highly scaled operation from a service provider. Private utilities are possible (though very different from a shared-services organization, which we'll discuss later) but incredibly difficult to create and manage.

We believe that no more than 10 percent of the global one thousand and largest government organizations in the world have sufficient scale internally to compete with the scale of large external providers with standardized offerings. Because of a lack of governance, however, most of these companies and organizations still won't be able to achieve the standardization necessary for scale economies. A successful private utility depends on standardization, just as external service providers do. Thus, most organizations that attempt to create private utilities end up with a shared-services organization (whether internal or external) that provides customized services to a variety of internal customers and fails to achieve cost competitiveness with truly standardized alternatives.

Customization and standardization have benefits and costs. The ongoing costs of standardization can be much lower, but don't underestimate the initial costs of adapting to standardized delivery. While customization requires less change from existing ways of doing things, and perhaps offers the promise of competitive differentiation, ongoing costs will be higher and could be much higher in the future. This is the lesson that many in IT learned from the highly customized environments created in the 1970s and 1980s and still in use today. Such systems, built when there were no packaged solutions available, may have once been regarded as the crown jewels of the organization. But now they have been matched or exceeded by off-the-shelf equivalents available in the market. In-house-developed systems, often called legacy systems, largely have moved from being assets to liabilities, because of the complexity of upgrading and integrating them. Outsourcing their maintenance may be difficult and will certainly be expensive—few service providers today want to take on additional custom-application work.

Aside from the problems that legacy systems pose to a sourcing strategy, their history offers us a lesson. As you consider contracting for a highly customized service that might deliver profound initial impact, return on investment, and competitive advantage, also consider that the service may become tomorrow's millstone—an expensive, nondifferentiated process that is now a liability. The sustainability of the differentiation of a service or process needs to be judged against the future costs and implications of attempting to build it through a customized approach.

The decision about standardized versus customized services must include the input of the COO, business unit heads, and the chief information officer (CIO) at a minimum. The COO and business unit heads must come to consensus on the level of standardization that is acceptable and agree to adhere to the standards. The CIO needs to inform other executives about the impacts of standardization on technology architecture and technology integration.

Finally, standardization versus customization is not just a binary decision. We presented it as such because it helps bring the relevant issues into stark relief and forces the necessary parties to really engage in the choices that are necessary. Ultimately, the choice here is one of degrees: exactly how much customization is needed and useful, considering the additional expense that customization requires. Of course, you also have the option of explicitly specifying that the service provider, internal or external, will take over a customized delivery model that exists today and move it to a standardized delivery model over time, with resulting decreases in cost. This popular choice often breaks down, though, when the service recipient fails to follow the agreed-to schedule for accepting standardization.

Once you have specified the delivery model that your organization requires for the desired service's outcomes, you need to consider one of the most politically sensitive questions of current business operations: where should the service be performed?

Question 3: Where Should the Service Be Performed?

A S W E H A V E D I S C U S S E D , outsourcing can be an extremely emotional and political issue. In this highly charged environment, outsourcing and offshoring have become wrongly conflated. *Outsourcing* implies nothing about where the work is performed; similarly, *offshoring* implies nothing about who is performing the work. Therefore, in general, we will use the terms domestic and nondomestic to avoid confusion. Because of all the attention paid to Indian, Chinese, and other locations, many organizations have been caught up asking the wrong questions when building their sourcing initiatives. They ask, "What should we be doing in India?" or "What's our China strategy?" While these are appropriate questions in looking at product strategy, given the growth of those economies, from a service perspective the real question is, "Does location matter?" In considering the answer to this question, we must evaluate a number of criteria.

People Intensiveness

The growth of global sourcing has been based primarily on lower labor costs for equivalent quality of personnel. While low labor cost is not the only reason to consider nondomestic sourcing, it is a significant part of the equation. Thus, the first issue to consider when evaluating the location dependency of a service is people intensiveness, or, does this service require a relatively large amount of human capital? For example, call centers are people intensive, while payroll processing is not. The more people intensive a process or service is, the more location dependent that service will be. Specifically, for maximum value, the service should be located where the organization can minimize personnel costs while maintaining the required quality.

People intensiveness, though, is not just about numbers; it's also about the availability of capabilities. The necessary capabilities for a service may not be available in every locality, and therefore, the location dependency is high. Don't assume, however, that a requirement for specialized skills means that a service has to be located in an industrialized country. Increasingly, organizations are turning to nondomestic services because the highly skilled personnel are often more available in low-wage countries than they are in industrialized nations.

Additionally, you need to consider the impact of automation on the people intensiveness of a service. Call centers, while still requiring many human beings, are much less people intensive than they used to be, because of advances in telephony technology. Similarly, software application development will become dramatically more automated over the next five years. Just because a process is people intensive today does not mean that it will be so tomorrow. Making a low-wage choice because of people costs today may not make sense three years from now, but the costs of entering into offshore operations internally or through a service provider will already have been spent.

Relationship Requirements

The next set of factors to consider relates to how tight the relationship between service recipient and provider needs to be and how much communication is required. Some organizations reject nondomestic options simply because of distance; many others wrongly equate having a common language with having a common culture and are surprised by communication difficulties. Organizations must understand the depth of relationship building that needs to take place for clear understanding and mutual trust between parties.

The amount of relationship building required depends on how quantifiable and objectively measurable the inputs and outputs of the service are (of course, in talking about services sourcing, we are assuming the inputs and outputs are information rather than tangible goods). The more that qualitative measurement is required—where the question is not simply "Is the job done?" but "How well is the job done?"— the more that communication and other interactions will be necessary. Building relationships so that interactions are effective takes time. When the parties in the relationship are geographically distant, building those relationships takes more time and effort. When service inputs are easily and objectively quantifiable, communication between the parties tends to be much easier and require less up-front relationship building.

Of course, language and cultural distance also affect the ease of building relationships. Just because two people speak the same language does not mean they can make themselves mutually understood. Cultural factors also play a role. There are more than enough examples in marketing literature about cross-cultural communication faux pas, so we do not need to rehash them here.

If close relationships are necessary between recipient and provider, you must factor the time and cost of overcoming geographic, language, and cultural distance into the equation. The high cost of relationship building may determine that the service is location dependent and needs to be performed in a geographically and culturally close location. This may still be outside the national borders of the service recipient; U.S. companies may look to Canada, for instance, as an option.

Knowledge Transfer

A related factor in the location-dependency equation is the amount of knowledge transfer required. Even if a service's inputs and outputs are quantifiable, a nondomestic operation, internal or external, may require a great deal of knowledge transfer before it can provide the service. In these cases, geographic, language, and cultural distance can complicate knowledge transfer and overcome any cost savings realized from lower wages in the short term. This is especially true in highly people-intensive services—you won't need to transfer knowledge to just one individual, but many of them. While knowledge transfer costs do not scale linearly with the number of people involved, there are certainly incremental costs to be dealt with.

Security and Control

When evaluating the question "Does location matter?" you must also consider how much control the organization desires to maintain over the service and the security needs of the service. These two factors are especially important when you are handling sensitive intellectual property (IP) or trade secrets, confidential customer data, or information governed by regulatory requirements in different geographies. While there are specific IP-protection concerns in specific countries, do not assume that IP will necessarily be safe in some places rather than others without performing some investigation. For example, many pundits have talked about the risk of ID theft through the processing of sensitive financial data in India. As of March 2005, however, more documented cases of ID theft were perpetrated or abetted by employees in the United States than by employees in low-wage countries. Again, the point is not that certain locations are safer than others, but that decision makers must evaluate each situation before assuming what the answers are.

You also need to consider regulatory requirements and privacy controls country by country. Regulatory requirements from a variety of governments may necessitate maintaining close audit controls on processes, people, and information. Moreover, the criticality of a process may lead executives to want direct, personal oversight of some services. In both cases, these factors may dictate a specific location for services to be provided.

Geopolitical Risk-Management Experience

Another factor for consideration is the geopolitical risk-management experience an organization has. Sourcing services from a variety of locations around the globe requires organizations to add geopolitical risk management to their stable of risk-management practices. In our experience, few organizations currently have the experience, knowledge, or processes to deal with geopolitical risks. Consequently, if an organization is considering nondomestic sourcing, it needs to acquire these skills. We want to be careful to avoid the hype of geopolitical risk that many naysayers of offshore sourcing espouse. There are, however, inherent and different risks to sourcing services in other countries. If you are sourcing a highly strategic service from India, China, Brazil, or Hungary, you need to have processes in place to monitor potential threats to the delivery of the service. That means monitoring elections, changes in executive and legislative power, labor unions, other internal politics, and regulatory stances as well as the international relations of those countries. How much geopolitical risk management you need depends, of course, on how critical the service is and how much it will cost you if disruptions occur.

Integration Complexity and Dependencies

Finally, you need to consider the integration complexity and dependencies of any service when evaluating its location dependency. You must consider not only the services and processes that create inputs or rely on outputs from the service, but also who provides the inputs and who consumes the outputs, where these parties are, and whether they are internal or external. Remember that you have to deal with the realities of Multisourcing—multiple providers and many service consumers. We discussed earlier the relationships you may have to build to effectively obtain services, but other parties (such as external service providers) may also have to build relationships. These parties may not have the same willingness or capability to build relationships and to work with geographically or culturally distant operations. On the other hand, you may already be sourcing some services, or doing business in some target geographies. If you move the provision of service to these countries, the integration complexity may decline. In fact, there is a powerful argument that most large organizations will have to have business operations in the rapidly growing economies of Brazil, India, and China; you can get a jumpstart on building successful business operations in these countries by gaining experience through locating service providers (internal or external) there first.

Recognizing the complexities of nondomestic service provision and the need to gain experience and new competencies in managing nondomestic providers led IndyMac Bank to pursue a phased approach to business process and IT nondomestic sourcing. The bank has a strategic plan to progressively pursue increasingly complex services from both captive and outsourced nondomestic providers over time as it gains expertise. The organization began exploring nondomestic opportunities to support the rapid growth in business due to the U.S. refinancing boom that began in late 2001. The first services IndyMac moved off-shore were basic loan-servicing call-center operations (for example, an introductory call to borrowers to explain the payment process). Simple loan-servicing data-entry tasks were added next, and in 2004, more complex back-office loan-processing functions were migrated. In mid-2004, IndyMac added IT outsourcing to its nondomestic strategy including application development, project management, and help desk, among other services. Future services under consideration include all central corporate-support functions. Mark Nelson, executive vice president of Global Resources, a position IndyMac created in 2004 to oversee this process, among others, believes that this measured approach to nondomestic sourcing has been just right. "Although our program grew to about 400 offshore personnel in its first year, we have taken measured steps, building on our experience with each new migration. Jumping into offshore with both feet, when we didn't have the experience to manage all the issues, would have been a big mistake. We've learned a lot during this process, and that's enabled us to meet our goals at each stage."[3]

A consideration of all the factors related to the location of services will help you determine the location dependency of each of your services. Possible answers range from "must be located domestically," to "must be located in a low-wage country," to "must be located geographically close to service recipient," to "is completely location independent." Assign each of the services on your map to one of these categories. The next step in building your service action plan is to determine whether these services, regardless of location, should be provided internally or externally.

Question 4: Should This Service Be Retained Internally or Outsourced?

THE FOURTH STEP, the question that most enterprises erroneously consider first, is to look at whether the service should be performed internally or sourced externally. Far too many organizations try to begin forming their sourcing strategy with this question and inevitably run off the rails.

To answer the questions of insourcing versus outsourcing, you must start with your business and sourcing maxims. As we noted, those maxims need to express what competencies are strategic to the organization, the enterprise view of sourcing risks, and the organization's general stance toward its human capital. These are your guardrails in evaluating each service. However, you'll also need to return to the discovery process and dig into each service more deeply than you did during the maxims process.

Before considering whether to insource or outsource the service, you need a detailed baseline of each service's current situation. This will involve determining service costs, current service levels, internal competence levels, and a capital asset inventory.

Establish the Baseline

Don't go into establishing baselines believing it will be easy. For most organizations, this is the most difficult and time-consuming part of creating a sourcing action plan. It is impossible to make good sourcing decisions without good baselines, though. There are four elements of your baseline for each service: service level, service costs, human capital assets, and other assets.

Service Level

You will have the beginning of the answer to current service levels if you properly identified the specified outcomes earlier in the process. Here you need to get specific about the exact levels of service being delivered in support of those outcomes (how many calls are being received, how many employees are being paid, how much network bandwidth is available?). Of course, your current service level may be underachieving or overachieving the expected outcomes. At this stage, you must note not just the business need and expectation but the current real service level being provided. Again these statements need to be in terms of outcomes—stating service levels as outcomes will allow you to make comparisons; stating service levels in enterprise-specific terms will make effective comparisons of different providers nearly impossible.

Service Cost

Your baseline needs to specify exactly what the current service costs are today and what the expected costs are over the planning horizon. If you've already outsourced this service or it is being provided by a shared-services organization, you will be ahead of the game, as current costs should be relatively easy to obtain. Don't forget, of course, to consider the outcomes expected of this service in the future. Will you need to invest in this service to bring it up to what the business needs? Have you made capital investments that will drive down the ongoing costs of meeting expectations? Will the costs of delivering this service rise or fall over the planning horizon? Many organizations fail to consider the future costs of human capital in these assessments. You need to consider whether the human capital involved in providing this service is a scarce resource. If it is, you will need to invest incrementally more in salary and other rewards to maintain service levels.

Human Capital Assets

This is the stage at which you will need to invest in detailed competency evaluations for your personnel. If you do not already have experience in creating competency categories and evaluating these competencies, we highly recommend engaging experts to assist you in this process. One of the significant benefits of engaging third-party experts is that their experience will enable the creation of competency inventories that can be compared to industry or service standards. If you do all this work yourself, that is, creating custom competency lists, you may again have trouble drawing meaningful comparisons.

Keep in mind that performing a competency inventory for current personnel can create a lot of angst. During this process, you will need to invoke your communications capability, keeping the employees informed about where you are in the sourcing strategy process, why you are performing this inventory, what decisions have been made (none at this stage), and what the expected timeline for making decisions is. The good news is that your best employees will generally welcome a competency inventory, as it will give them an opportunity to objectively demonstrate their value. This perspective, however, is entirely dependent on evaluating your employees against the right competencies. Your best employees will be the first to recognize if your competency lists are inadequate or misdirected or if your measurement process is invalid, and they will file out the door faster than you can imagine. This is yet another reason to engage outside help if you are not completely confident in your internal capabilities to get this right.

Other Assets

Finally, you'll need to consider what physical assets and knowledge assets (such as process or industry best practices) you have. Physical assets include owned equipment, equipment leases, software licenses, and facilities, among other categories. Process or industry knowledge unique to your organization should be categorized also. Both sets of assets will be important in creating the business case for your sourcing decisions, which we will discuss later in this chapter.

Benchmark Your Baseline

With this baseline established, you will need to benchmark your baseline against the broader market. In some cases, and in most cases for business processes, you will want to benchmark against others in your industry. At other times, you will want to benchmark against the general market. This benchmark will give you objective information on how your current situation compares to others. This information is critical because it is the only way to know what your current competence and skill is for the service in question. Without external benchmarking, you will have no way to confirm whether your current provider (internal or external) is doing well or poorly in delivering this service and whether you are over- or underinvested in this service relative to your peers. Occasionally, benchmarking may not be necessary—primarily when the organization knows that it performs very poorly. Do not make the mistake of believing you perform well without benchmarking; most organizations we talk to significantly overestimate their performance in relation to industry or market benchmarks. The result of your benchmark is an objective measure of your competence in delivering service at an appropriate value.

Evaluate Services Based on Competence and Differentiation

The key to deciding what services should remain insourced and which you should consider outsourcing is the overlap between internal competence in the service and the service's differentiation value. This differentiation value might also be called core competence, following C. K. Prahalad and Gary Hamel's approach. We avoid using this terminology, because the ideas of core competence (what the organization must be good at to provide competitive differentiation and succeed in the market) and actual competence (what the organization can do well today) are often confused.

Your business maxims and sourcing maxims specify what services have high or low differentiation value to the enterprise (or specific business units). Your baseline and benchmarking establish your actual competence.

You can then measure each service being evaluated against the two axes depicted in figure 3-2. What quadrant they fall into based on this evaluation will guide you in your decision to insource or outsource. There is also a correlation with the three types of deals, which we've mapped to the right of the quadrants.

The lower left quadrant indicates those services for which your actual competence is low in relation to the market or industry and the differentiation value of the service is also low. This quadrant is the low-hanging fruit of outsourcing—clearly, you should be pursing opportunities to outsource these services (if you haven't done so already). Outsourcing of services in this quadrant is largely responsible for the proven benefits of outsourcing that led many companies to outsource services falling into the other quadrants without appreciating the critical differences in approach required for success.

FIGURE 3-2

Choosing insourcing or outsourcing

The decision to insource or outsource a particular service depends on its differentiation value and your organization's current competence at providing it.

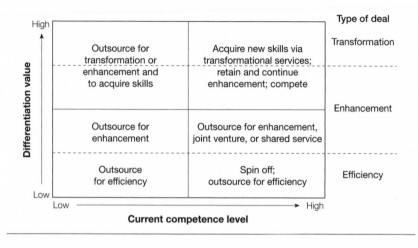

In the upper left quadrant are services that have a high differentiation and strategic value to the organization but that the organization performs poorly. Here again, outsourcing is the preferred option, but for very different reasons. For services in this quadrant, you will be seeking outsourcers that are best in class at these services and that can transform the service provision while transferring knowledge and skills to you. Ultimately, as your internal competence improves, you may want to bring this service in-house; this is not a foregone conclusion, but you will want to structure a deal that provides this option.

In the lower right corner are those services for which your internal competence is high but that deliver low differentiation value. There are a variety of ways in which this circumstance comes about. Sometimes, the services have provided differentiation in the past but the market has caught up. Occasionally, an organization has to build a capability internally because no market sources are available. In the worst situations, the capability has been allowed to reach unneeded levels of competence without being checked for return on investment.

For services within this quadrant, the first option is to consider spinning off or selling this capability to a third party (recall the ChemCo example in Chapter 2). There is a very good chance that the service may be more valuable to a service provider or another organization for which this service is the focus of its differentiation. Another alternative is to look at investing in the capability, via outsourcing or internally, to transform or enhance the service so that it does provide differentiation.

The final quadrant, the upper right, is the domain of services that will remain inside. These are services that the organization excels at providing and that are necessary for competitive differentiation. You will continue to invest in maintaining and enhancing this capability internally; you may consider using outsourcing as a mechanism for maintaining or enhancing this competence if there are service providers that can assist in this process (although there may well not be).

Choose Sourcing Relationship Options

Part of choosing "in or out" is determining the relationship option appropriate for the specific service. We've identified eight sourcing relationship models that fulfill different needs.[4] Every model presents a different relationship balance between service recipient and service providers, which can be external providers or internal providers (i.e., with insourcing). These relationship models will become critical parts of selecting providers, which we'll cover in chapter 5.

Traditionally, there were only two sourcing models: insource and outsource. However, today's competitive world requires a far greater array of choices that recognize the dynamic needs of the organization and the interplay of internal and external capabilities as well as the relationships between external providers.

Enterprise needs have forced an evolution of relationship options away from binary choices; full-service outsourcing (in which an entire horizontal operation, such as IT or finance, is outsourced to a single provider) has declined. Organizations are generally less willing to completely dismantle internal operations and transfer their capabilities and assets externally, because of the high costs involved in switching to another provider in the future. Service recipients are also learning that effective management requires that some capabilities and competencies, and therefore some staff, stay in-house. On a cost analysis, we've found that full single-source outsourcing can be up to 50 percent more expensive than the market average for such services and still not provide the organization with satisfactory services or innovation.

The relationship models described hereafter fall into two categories—insourced models and outsourced models. Using your decisions about outcomes, customization, location, and internal versus external delivery, you'll choose between them for each service. Remember that in the multisourced world, you'll use several, if not all, of these models simultaneously for the delivery of different services. We present the models in the order of progressively greater access to best-in-class capabilities and progressively less control of service delivery (figure 3-3).

Insourcing Option: Internal Delivery

Internal delivery describes the provision of services by internal personnel without attempts to standardize service delivery across business

FIGURE 3-3

Sourcing relationship options

Today's enterprises can select from a variety of sourcing relationships, with different levels of control and access to best-in-class capabilities.

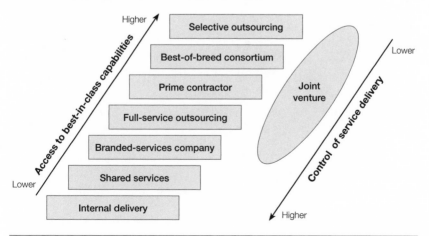

units or geographies. For example, each business unit would have its own HR function and personnel. These functions would operate independently, with little or no cooperation or leverage of synergies and processes. Of all the options, this one provides the most control of service delivery, because the rules and processes that shape service delivery can be changed as much and as often as needed. It is also the most limited sourcing option with regard to scale and process knowledge. Internal delivery corresponds to the *build* sourcing action.

Insourcing Option: Shared Services

The shared-services option creates, in essence, an internal company to deliver services to the whole organization. The key distinguishing feature of the shared-services option is that this internal company operates its own profit and loss statement and, via some mechanism, such as chargeback, recoups its cost of operations from the business units that access its services. For instance, finance may be a shared service, with every business unit or region paying for access to the same resources to perform the finance function. If separation and cost recovery is not used, then the service would qualify as internal delivery, not shared services.

The advantage of a shared-services option is that it can help provide standardization, limited scale, and lower costs compared with internal delivery. Organizations also maintain a high degree of control and can, with relative ease compared with other options, provide customization of services when business requirements dictate. In addition, a shared-services option can help an organization discover the real costs of a service and uncover the true ways that work gets done. On the negative side, shared-services organizations don't provide the scale necessary to reach the lowest possible price points and require strong enterprise governance to enforce standardization and cost recovery. Many organizations use the shared-services option as a first step toward considering outsourcing because it reveals costs and management issues before involving a third party. Shared services is a blend of the *build* and *compete* sourcing action categories.

Insourcing Option: Branded-Services Company

A branded-services company is a step beyond the shared-services option. With branded services, the shared-services organization offers its services to the market at large, not just the organization that sponsors it. Clearly, a branded-services company offers the potential for greater access to scale and lower costs to the service recipient, as overhead costs are spread even wider. However, many shared-services operations that have tried to become branded-services companies have found that adding sales, marketing, and true customer-service capability is much harder and more expensive than anticipated. Additionally, the parent company often becomes uncomfortable with the loss of control that occurs when a branded-services company has to respond to its other customers' needs. The vast majority of enterprises that have tried branded services have retrenched. Some of today's well-known external service providers, however, began as branded-services companies. For example, ISSC, the predecessor to IBM Global Services, began as a spin-off of IBM's internal IS operation, and CGI began as a spin-off of Bell Canada's IS operation. The branded services company corresponds to the *compete* sourcing action

Outsourcing Option: Full-Service Outsourcing

The full-service outsourcing option is the classic outsourcing model that predominated in the 1980s and for most of the 1990s. In this option, an organization signs a single contract with a single external service provider for the provision of all the functions within a category of services. For instance, the organization would outsource the entire IT function (as opposed to contracting for application maintenance and network management independently). In the 1980s and early 1990s, full outsourcing was used extensively for IT. The adoption of this option, however, has decreased in a maturing market in which competition has increased. For BPO, full outsourcing is a preferred option in cases of significant asset transfer and complex, integrated processes. In a low-maturity marketplace, this also is driven by providers specializing in a defined set of bundled processes.

MAKING THE FULL-SERVICE CHOICE: QUALEX

Qualex, a wholly owned subsidiary of Eastman Kodak Company that focuses on photo processing for consumers in the United States and Canada, faced a quandary. Due to massive changes in the photography industry brought on by the advent of mass-market digital photography, the company needed to drastically cut costs across its business. Qualex's IT function had been outsourced to a full-service provider for nearly a decade—service and the relationship with the provider were both very strong, but the contract and the cost structure were no longer effective.

Chris Jones, director of information systems at Qualex, says the organization faced a difficult choice: "We could either negotiate with the incumbent provider and try to bring our costs down while maintaining our strong relationship, or we could rebid the services and go after maximum cost savings via selective outsourcing, and take the risk on a new and unproven supplier relationship."[a]

Qualex engaged the incumbent in a four-month process to develop a complete statement of work that could be used for a request for a proposal (RFP) later if necessary, and to create detailed baselines of Qualex's current IT portfolio. Using that document, Qualex entered

---

Full-service outsourcing provides the benefits of access to scale and less complex management versus using multiple providers that have to interface with each other (see "Making the Full-Service Choice: Qualex"). On the negative side, full outsourcing limits access to best-in-class capabilities (no service provider will be best in class at everything) and increases delivery risk (if the single provider fails to invest to improve its capabilities or suffers other business failures, there are no easy alternatives to turn to). Full-service outsourcing corresponds to the *buy* sourcing action.

Outsourcing Option: Prime Contractor

The prime-contractor option relies on a single provider to manage service delivery but accesses multiple providers to actually deliver the

negotiations with the service provider to completely restructure the contract. "Our goal was not just to bring costs down but to make sure that costs were able to move up and down based on business need. Given the amount of change in the industry, we couldn't be locked into fixed costs for IT services," says Jones.

Qualex benchmarked the statement of work and pricing against industry averages to provide important input to the negotiation process. While negotiations were unsurprisingly tough, the strong relationship that already existed allowed Qualex and the provider to arrive at mutually agreeable statements of work and terms and conditions.

On the basis of all the inputs, Qualex concluded that staying with the incumbent in a full-service outsourcing arrangement made the most sense. "It came down to risk versus savings. The strong relationship we had with the incumbent was the deciding factor for us," says Jones. "No new provider would be able to match the incumbent's deep knowledge of our business and our effective processes for managing the deal together."

a. Chris Jones, director of information services, Qualex, telephone interview with authors, March 29, 2005.

services. In this case, the organization contracts with an external service provider to deliver a set of services, but dictates that this service provider find and engage other service providers to provide best-in-class capabilities across the range of services being accessed. With this option, the service recipient does not specify which service providers will be used; this decision rests with the prime contractor. The prime-contractor option improves on the full-service outsourcing option by providing improved access to capabilities. It also decreases the service delivery risk associated with the failure of the prime contractor or any of the individual subcontractors. This option, however, does increase the complexity risk—the prime contractor may fail to act effectively as a manager and as a liaison between the service recipient and the subcontractors. The prime-contractor option corresponds to the *buy* sourcing action.

Outsourcing Option: Best-of-Breed Consortia

This option differs from the prime-contractor option in that the service recipient specifies exactly who the providers are for each aspect of the service. Rather than taking on the management of each service provider, the service recipient requires all the service providers to come together and create a single management interface. The best-of-breed option first appeared in the market in the 1990s as an evolution of full-service outsourcing for very large deals involving large, multinational organizations. The consortium option today most often is a result of a recipient's desire to package together a group of services that cannot be provided by any single existing provider. Typically, only large, private and government entities have the leverage to create consortia, but once these consortia are formed, they often market their services to others— again in an effort to achieve scale.

Accessing best-in-class capabilities via a consortium affords the recipient greater control over service delivery than does the prime-contractor option without requiring that the recipient assume much more management responsibility. Other risks, however, such as the inability of the service providers to cooperate (given that they are essentially being forced to cooperate with providers that they often compete with) and choosing the wrong set of providers, increase. Best-of-breed consortia correspond to the *buy* sourcing action.

Outsourcing Option: Selective Outsourcing

The next option is selective outsourcing, in which the service recipient takes on choosing and managing each provider. Today, this is the most used approach for IT outsourcing. Although selective outsourcing often seems to make the most intuitive sense (i.e., it is the selection of the best provider for a given need), it is the most difficult sourcing option to manage. Rather than managing a single provider that in turn handles the management of other providers, the recipient is managing multiple providers. Selective outsourcing means that the recipient has to take on the role of integrator and fill any gaps in service delivery internally or by contracting with additional providers. In addition, the service recipient is the primary risk owner, especially regarding problems that span multiple providers or when disputes and finger pointing among providers occur. Many organizations have chosen selective out-sourcing by accident—because they don't have a sourcing strategy, they create a selective outsourcing environment through ad hoc, disconnected sourcing decisions.

Selective outsourcing can help ensure that the organization is accessing the best capabilities at the best price (as long as competition is encouraged by the selection process). However, the management costs that the organization incurs are higher. Potentially, this option can provide the best of everything, but it requires extensive experience and sophisticated management of sourcing to function well. Selective out-sourcing falls in the *buy* sourcing action category

Outsourcing Option: Joint Venture

When very rapid change is necessary, or when a provider has unique capabilities, or under other special circumstances (see "A Successful Joint Venture in Practice: Ontario Power Generation"), a joint venture is an option. Joint ventures are difficult to categorize, because the option involves two or more parties and a wide variety of contract terms. The term *joint venture* is often used interchangeably with the terms *alliance* or *partnership*. We define a joint venture as the creation, by two or more partners, of a new business entity. The single, most compelling reason to form a joint venture is for the partners to leverage their relevant unique capabilities to get to market and achieve change in a very short time. The value of the joint venture is often based on one partner's ver-tical or industry expertise and another partner's technical capabilities.

Many joint-venture operations ultimately fail to meet expectations. The most common reasons are misalignment of objectives, lack of focus by the parties, conflicting management interests, and a lack of exit planning. Several critical success factors must be present for a joint venture to flourish and deliver the intended value to the partners involved. They include mutual opportunity, strategic value, cultural fit, trust and due diligence, effective joint governance, sales and marketing, and appropriate funding. Joint ventures correspond to the *cooperate* sourcing action.

A SUCCESSFUL JOINT VENTURE IN PRACTICE: ONTARIO POWER GENERATION

The joint-venture sourcing option is best applied in special circumstances, like those facing Ontario Power Generation (OPG), a private power-generation company whose sole shareholder is the Ontario provincial government. In the mid-1990s, the government, following a path toward deregulation of the electricity industry, required OPG to lower its market share in the electricity-generating market. The company had to decontrol certain generating plants (either by selling or leasing the plants to third parties).

Since IT is a crucial part of the operation of power plants, it was impractical to sell plants without the IT systems and the staff needed to run them. OPG's large central IT infrastructure provided significant economies of scale, but would be very difficult to partition. Additionally, IT costs were expected to become significantly less competitive as OPG began to decontrol stations. The solution to these challenges yielded a joint venture with Capgemini to take on IT infrastructure for both OPG and for the plants that would be decontrolled. The joint venture, called New Horizon System Solutions, was structured to sell services to whoever took on the decontrolled plants as well as taking on the collective bargaining agreements covering unionized employees (a large portion of OPG's workforce is unionized in either the Power Workers Union or

Assembling Your Sourcing Choices

The sourcing relationship options you choose will have dramatic impacts on both your governance structure for each relationship and the provider selection process. Ultimately, these decisions should be guided by your organization's stance on risk, its need to maintain close control of delivery, its desire for access to scale, its desire for best-in-class service components, and its willingness to take on the necessary investments in sourcing management. As always, there are trade-offs—access to scale requires giving up some control; access to best-in-class the Society of Professional Employees). Capgemini took 51 percent ownership of the joint venture, while OPG held 49 percent. The board of New Horizon was equally split between the two companies.

The joint venture was not just a positive for OPG; Capgemini used the joint-venture approach to help mitigate risk, given the nature of the project and its limited experience in the area at the time. The terms of the joint venture dictated that Capgemini had to buy out OPG in two years or sell its share to OPG. Thus, both parties had needed goals met.

The deal worked so well that Capgemini bought out OPG after just one year. OPG continues to source the bulk of its IT services from New Horizon and achieves cost benefits, as New Horizon is also successfully selling its services to other clients, spreading its overhead over multiple contracts. Over time, the contract is also converting more costs to variable costs, another key goal of OPG. Dietmar Reiner, CIO for OPG, has been very pleased with the deal. "The joint venture set a great tone for building an ongoing relationship with New Horizon and Capgemini—we had to work together as business partners. Now OPG IT staff and New Horizon staff work together to meet business unit needs and find innovative solutions—and to show value to our mutual customers."[a]

a. Dietmar Reiner, chief information officer, Ontario Power Generation, telephone interview with authors, March 27, 2005.

services requires a greater investment in sourcing management competencies and governance. For each of the services in your map, designate whether it will be internal or external and which of the sourcing options is most appropriate for meeting business objectives.

You face one final step in crafting your action plan to move each service from where it is today to where your organization needs it to be tomorrow. You must build the business case that shows that your choices meet organizational requirements for cash flow and return on investment.

Question 5: Will My Service Choices Generate the Needed Return on Investment?

YOU MAY BE WONDERING why we have waited until this late stage to discuss the numbers side of the equation. Many people we work with on developing a sourcing strategy immediately want to know what the options cost: "How can I choose insource versus outsource if I don't know what each option costs?" is a frequently asked question. We recommend, however, that you hold the financial side of the discussion after you decide on the aforementioned questions, for several reasons. First, we have found that when financials enter the conversation too early, a thorough consideration of the possible options is curtailed. This omission tends to lead to future dissatisfaction among the parties to the decision, who may later question its validity. Second, by ensuring that all options are evaluated, and the theoretically optimal choice is made, you gain a better understanding of the needs of the organization and the expected intangible value to be created. Finally, until you have evaluated all the options, the potential cost factors are not clearly defined. Projecting future costs without specifying levels of customization, onshore or offshore sourcing, and sourcing relationship options creates far too fuzzy a picture for a rational decision.

Therefore, only after all the preceding questions are answered are we ready to consider the business case and the return on investment. Of course, the result of such an analysis often means that the choices have to be revisited. While you may desire a middle ground between customization and standardization, or to source services domestically, or to use a selective sourcing option, you may not be able to afford it. As you can see, this whole process is often circular, not linear. For many of the services you are evaluating, you will have to reconsider your earlier choices. This circular process helps all the people involved in the decision understand the trade-offs that they have to make.

Keep in mind that at this stage, the goal of the sourcing business case is not to look at exact dollar figures. Here you are determining whether the choices you have made make financial sense in general terms—whether or not it is worth pursuing further the options you believe are most appropriate for each service your organization needs. You will not know the final dollars and cents of a particular choice until you complete negotiations with a chosen source, internal or external. So, just as you may have to return to your sourcing options over and over, you will need to return often to your business case to update the figures as they become clearer through the processes of provider selection and negotiation.

The Challenge of Building a Sourcing Business Case

The two most common problems we see in sourcing business cases are the lack of standardization across service categories and incomplete consideration of the full costs of various sourcing choices.[5] Multisourcing requires thinking of all sourcing actions in the same terms—therefore a common business case model is needed to ensure decisions are made consistently. Good Multisourcing decisions, though, require that you consider all the costs of the various options before making any choices. When outsourcing deals fail to meet expectations, incomplete business cases are often the cause. Unanticipated costs dramatically increase the overall cost of the outsourcing relationship—the expected cost savings are never realized. Including all relevant costs in the analysis is, unfortunately, not easy.

Many companies have adopted a total-cost-of-ownership approach to managing their physical assets—considering not just up-front costs but ongoing management, maintenance, and opportunity costs. But when it comes to services, and particularly sourcing issues related to service delivery, most companies do not have the sophisticated cost models necessary for sound financial decision making. Some of the additional cost categories that most organizations fail to consider when creating their sourcing business case are these:

- *Governance costs:* Costs related to the service recipient's internal team and management processes for dealing with external service providers and internal stakeholders. These costs are different from the enterprise-level governance discussed in chapter 2, and we'll cover them in detail in chapter 4.

- *Tactical project costs:* Included are the project costs for executing the sourcing action plan: the selection of service providers and contract negotiation, and obtaining external advice (consultants, benchmarking, legal, etc.).

- *Transition costs:* These are costs incurred to move a service from its current service provider to the newly chosen provider. They include transition management, possible service interruptions or underperformance, training, and knowledge transfer.

- *Transfer costs:* Costs related to the transfer of assets, both physical and human capital assets, to a different service provider (terminating leases, asset price negotiation, staff severance and relocation, etc.).

Your business case for sourcing also needs to have a multiyear view of not only these costs, but all the costs involved in the current state. You must also provide a meaningful comparison with the status quo. Besides a linear projection of current costs, the comparison should show the investments necessary to ensure appropriate service delivery in the future. This relates to your earlier decisions about deal type: efficiency, enhancement, and transformation. Your sourcing business case cannot compare the current costs of a service that needs to be transformed with the costs of transformation via outsourcing. For the comparison to be valid, you need to estimate the internal cost of performing the same transformation.

Additionally, your sourcing business case should make some reasonable predictions of change. At a minimum, look at a three-year horizon. This will give your organization sufficient time to digest any effects of investments to its costs. Remember, as the list of often hidden costs shows, switching from one provider or one model to another takes considerable effort and is expensive.

Before we look at the specific components of a sourcing business case, we offer one final word of advice: make sure you are comparing apples to apples. Put another way, you can only compare sourcing options that deliver the same services at comparable service levels. If options are incomparable, then any finance discussions on the options will become fuzzy. This often happens when the evaluation allows service level creep, that is, the succumbing to the temptation of looking at service levels higher than are necessary to meet the business outcomes. Any money spent on service levels above what is necessary for business outcomes is wasted. When making price comparisons, never ask what service can be delivered—only determine the price of the required service levels (see "Financial Engineering").

Business Case Components

Your business case should compare the costs of the status quo to one or more sourcing options that are based on the choices you have made in the previous steps. The various cost elements to consider are ongoing costs (broken out by fixed and variable costs), capital and investment costs, tactical project costs, governance costs, transition costs, and transfer costs. We've modeled these cost categories for several options in table 3-1, showing the general type of costs in each category and their relation to each other across three sample options: internal delivery, shared services, and selective outsourcing. For example, in this sample scenario, transition costs for the internal delivery option are zero, as the service is currently provided in-house (but if a decision has been made to bring a previously outsourced service back in-house, then the opposite would be true).

Estimate the Costs of Various Options

Completing the business case requires estimating the costs for each category for each option. It will be impossible, of course, to know the exact costs that you can expect from options that you are not currently using. This can be particularly hard when you are trying to estimate the costs of outsourcing a particular service that is currently provided in-house.

Good information about costs is not easily available. Market prices, when available, are often poor indicators because the publicly quoted prices are contaminated with financial engineering, lack of inclusion of governance costs, unknown transformation costs, and unknown service provider motives (a low price may be the result of a service provider's

*F*inancial engineering is a term used to describe the manipulation of pricing to minimize the up-front costs of a deal. Historically initiated by the service provider (but today often initiated by the recipient), it entails tailoring the payment structure of a service relationship to make initial payments lower. This often appeals to the cash-flow needs or desires of the service recipient. Today, the most common reasons for financial engineering are associated with providers' "buying" capacity, expertise, or "referenceable" accounts to grow into a new service area, or with cash-strapped service recipients demanding cash concessions from providers.

Through financial engineering, the price of a service is no longer connected to the actual current cost of delivering the service. Typically, the service provider uses explicit or implicit financial loans that are not easily separated from service delivery costs. In this manner, a volatile cost pattern can be shaped toward a more balanced pattern. The benefits of the provider's investments are passed along earlier to the service recipient, and the costs of the investments are spread into coming years.

The use of financial engineering presents a number of problems for all parties. Service recipients face dramatically rising service prices at the back end of these deals, which may not always be apparent. Service providers are also at risk of having margins erode if the implicit loans are not repaid, a situation that can arise due to early renegotiation or client bankruptcy; this margin risk forces the service providers to resist contract changes or scope adjustments that are not entirely in their favor.

Your sourcing business case needs to be based on actual costs, whereas financial engineering depends on lots of assumptions about the future. You may later decide to use financial engineering to meet business cash flow and capital investment needs, but those needs should be considered separately in the evaluation. This is why it is important to use external, market-average benchmarks that help minimize the distorting effects of financial engineering in specific deals, rather than just gathering information anecdotally or directly from service providers when you are estimating costs. As noted, the business case needs to compare apples to apples; financial engineering distorts the comparisons if these details are not separated from actual cost figures. By considering actual costs as well as the potential cash-flow benefits of financial engineering separately, you will identify the real total costs involved in your sourcing decisions. This will also lessen confusion at the negotiating table.

TABLE 3-1

Business case components

The various cost categories used in building a business case with relative costs and major cost components for three sourcing options. The example assumes that the service being evaluated is currently performed internally.

Cost categories	Status quo, or internal delivery	Shared services	Selective outsourcing
Ongoing costs (fixed and variable)	Annualized current baseline; mostly fixed costs	Estimated costs from external benchmarking, generally lower, mostly fixed costs	Estimated costs and external benchmarking, generally lowest; higher percentage of variable costs
Capital and investment costs	Projected costs to attain future business goals	Projected costs to attain future business goals from external benchmarking	Projected costs to attain future business goals from external benchmarking, generally lower
Tactical project costs	N/A	Consultants, bench-marking, negotiation team	Consultants, additional benchmarking, higher negotiation costs
Governance costs	Current costs from baseline and invest-ment required to meet expectations	Costs related to new model: standardization, relationship managers, education and training for service recipients	Costs related to new model: investment in sourcing management competencies, creating operational service levels, additional staff to manage service provider interaction and multiple contracts
Transition costs	N/A	Staff redeployment, training, hiring; possible service interruptions	Knowledge transfer, possible service interruptions
Transfer costs	N/A	Asset transfer and personnel transfer	Asset transfer and personnel transfer

"buying" its way into a particular industry, geography, or class of service). In building a business case, some organizations approach the market to collect bids, but this process is not necessarily reliable and can start relationships with service providers off on the wrong foot (a topic we'll discuss more in chapter 5).

One way to obtain useful financial data for building business cases and evaluating options is to engage consultants that specialize in benchmarking or negotiating outsourcing relationships or law firms with similar specialties. You are looking for a firm that has handled many contracts and therefore can provide a realistic estimate of the costs of achieving your business outcomes via your delivery, location, and sourcing relationship choices. Again, you are not looking to assess the exact dollars and cents of the options but to provide a reasonable price range to justify pursuing one or more options further.

Consider Cash Flow and Variable Costs

Creating and analyzing the business case options will often require sophisticated financial modeling so that the true and complete costs and benefits can be understood. The quality of your business case will often depend on the quality of the financial experts you have working with you. Two factors that require close attention in your cost modeling are cash flow and variable costs. One of many benefits of outsourcing has been its impact on these two factors.

Many executives, without considering all the factors involved, perceive outsourcing solely in these terms. Additionally, there is the perception that outsourcing a service will allow a movement from fixed costs to variable costs based on the need for the service. Outsourcing does sometimes change costs from fixed to variable: when the organization's needs decline, the cost of obtaining the service through an external provider may also decline. This is certainly not true in an insourced scenario—personnel costs and asset costs are fixed, no matter how demand for a service fluctuates. Note that these perceived benefits of outsourcing are not guaranteed; they have more or less impact, depending on the models that are chosen and the contracts that are signed. This is why it's so important to factor in these assumptions and create multiple scenarios to model their effects.

Nonfinancial Factors of Your Sourcing Maxims

While working on your sourcing business cases, you may begin viewing your choices only in terms of financials. Of course, the choices must take into account nonfinancial drivers as well. This is why you created sourcing maxims—to recognize all the business reasons, not just the financial ones, for your sourcing decisions. Your maxims may dictate choices that are more expensive than alternatives. As you prepare your business case, you will want to refer back to your sourcing maxims often, to ensure that the real criteria for the enterprise's sourcing decisions are recognized there and are being taken into account.

Additionally, you need to consider risk stance as it is captured in your maxims. All sourcing includes risk—the risks simply vary by what sourcing options are chosen and how deeply your organization internalizes the discipline of Multisourcing. The costs of managing risk are an important part of the business case. In making sourcing decisions, your organization needs to recognize the costs of managing the risks introduced by your choices, but also the savings from reducing risks by making these same choices. For instance, if you decide to use multiple best-in-class service providers, your risk of inadequate service declines, but your risk from sourcing complexity increases. The costs and benefits of this changing mix of risks should be considered.

You may find, however, that when it comes to the actual cost differences or risk differences between sourcing options, some executives' feelings on the enterprise's sourcing maxims may change. We must reiterate that the decision process is cyclical and will require you to circle back to the beginning, even all the way back to your sourcing maxims. This cyclical process ensures that a view of real cost implications doesn't change executives' and business unit leaders' views of the proper theoretical approaches (as represented in maxims and other choices in the sourcing strategy process). This is why it is so crucial to create governance mechanisms for evaluating and revising sourcing maxims and sourcing choices, as information gained during the sourcing strategy process may require review of prior decisions.

This Is Your Sourcing Strategy

ONCE YOU'VE ANSWERED the five questions for each of your services from your current map, you can create your future map of Multisourcing. The set of answers for each service is your sourcing action plan for that service, guiding you on any changes that need to be made.

The sum of your sourcing action plans is your sourcing strategy. As you create a consensus action plan within the framework of your maxims and the governance mechanisms you chose in chapter 2, remember the importance of documenting the choices that have been made and their rationale. You will need to refer to these repeatedly during provider selection and contract negotiation. You'll continue to refer to those decisions over time as you review your sourcing strategy yearly and assess your success. For each service, you may want to create a map that indicates the choices made and the journey that the action plan requires. Tables 3-2 and 3-3 show what the map for the example company in chapter 1 looks like before and after taking into account the organization's sourcing action plans.

Let's look at a couple of the services to explain the changes. Although the organization has decided to fully spin off the joint venture

TABLE 3-2

Old Multisourcing map

	Sourcing actions	Global sourcing options	Four worlds	Types of deals
Finance	Cooperate	In-house, domestic and captive, nondomestic	Optimization	Enhancement
Benefits	Buy	Outsource, domestic	Optimization	Efficiency
Payroll	Buy	Outsource, domestic	Management	Efficiency
Human resources	Compete	In-house, domestic	Optimization	Enhancement
Data network	Buy	Outsource, domestic	Management	Efficiency
Data center	Build	In-house, domestic	Management	Efficiency
Enterprise applications	Build	Captive, domestic	Optimization	Efficiency
Call center	Build	In-house, domestic and nondomestic	Optimization	Transformation

TABLE 3-3

New Multisourcing map, with sourcing action plans

	Sourcing actions	Global sourcing options	Four worlds	Types of deals
Finance	Buy, prime contractor	Outsource, domestic and offshore	Optimization	Efficiency
Benefits and payroll	Buy, full service	Outsource, domestic	Optimization	Efficiency
Human resources	Compete	Insource, via captive nondomestic operation	Creation	Enhancement
Data network	Buy, selective outsourcing	Outsource, domestic and nondomestic	Management	Efficiency
Data center	Buy, prime contractor	Outsource, domestic and (nearshore) nondomestic	Access	Enhancement
Enterprise applications	Build/buy, selective outsourcing	All options used	Optimization/ Access	Enhancement
Call center	Buy	In-house, captive nondomestic	Optimization	Efficiency

it formed for finance, it will continue to purchase services from this entity. The organization expects that the performance gains it achieved in forming the joint venture will be stabilized and the provider will now focus on bringing costs down—thus the deal will move from enhancement to efficiency. The company has decided to outsource the data center and to seek performance enhancement—spending will remain stable as the cost savings from outsourcing will be plowed into paying for service enhancement. At the same time, internal IT staff will be put in place to manage data center services to ensure business value. Enterprise applications, on the other hand, will be split between internal and external resources so that appropriate focus can be delivered to applications that provide the most business value.

In closing, remember that a sourcing strategy is a dynamic entity that must be reassessed as the business needs, strategies, and executives change. Any major shift in business operations or strategy will demand a realignment of the sourcing strategy to the business strategy.

Your organization will need to reassess the viable sourcing alternatives and refresh the business case for sourcing to reflect the most viable alternatives, given the new set of circumstances. If change occurs to the business, then the sourcing strategy must change, as the purpose of a Multisourcing discipline is to provide the services that lead to the outcomes that will help your organization realize its strategic aims.

four

Govern and Manage Multisourcing

IN CHAPTER 2, WE INTRODUCED THE THREE ELEMENTS of sourcing governance—maxims, initiatives, and management—and the sourcing council, a body responsible for sourcing maxims and overseeing the other sourcing governance elements. Before continuing further, we need to return to the topic of governance and discuss the central importance of governance to Multisourcing. Further on in the chapter, we'll discuss sourcing management governance specifically and the management techniques that flow out of good sourcing governance.

Although the day-to-day activity of Multisourcing management occurs after service providers (internal or external) are chosen, the decision rights, rules, processes, and approaches for management must be defined before the providers are engaged. Governance is at the heart of Multisourcing. You cannot build successful sourcing relationships, internally or externally, until you have set up sourcing governance models appropriate to Multisourcing and funded them according to your risk-management approach.

Part I: Governing Multisourcing

S OURCING GOVERNANCE establishes both the common and the unique approaches for managing the varying mix of internal and external service providers that characterizes Multisourcing. Specifically, sourcing governance is the assignment of rights and responsibilities for all decisions regarding the use and management of internally and externally provided resources and services, with the objective of upholding the organization's sourcing maxims, assuring service coordination, and achieving business results.

Multisourcing requires both common, standardized approaches to sourcing issues and clear rules for the few exceptions. Without standardized, well-understood management processes, agility is impossible. Creating a dynamic mix of sources requires that all the providers adhere to the same approaches and rules so that decisions can be made and implemented quickly. Governance is central to creating these standardized processes and approaches. Additionally, sourcing governance allows enterprise-level views of the organization's sourcing health by establishing common and comparable metrics for sourcing relationships. Finally, sourcing governance creates a structure for individual service relationships to thrive and deliver expected results even in a changing environment by creating processes to ensure productive relationship management.

We need to note first, though, that governance is not about organizational charts, but about roles and responsibilities. As we discuss the tasks of governance and management, do not equate tasks or roles with a particular job. One person may perform many of the tasks and roles. Every organization needs to perform all the roles and tasks we describe, but each organization needs to map those roles and tasks to its own organization chart. There is no "right" way to organize to accomplish these tasks.

What Is Sourcing Governance?

Neglect of sourcing governance is a contributing factor in almost every case of sourcing chaos that we help clients bring under control. Far too many organizations assume that putting relationship or service managers in place is a substitute for governance. Chaos results when these managers realize that there are no clear rules about who has authority to make what decisions.

Governance is about authority: how decisions are made, who gets to make them, and who's accountable for the decisions. Management is about responsibility—responsibility for delivering to expectations. Governance involves input and the decision rights to drive desirable behaviors, whereas management means making and implementing specific decisions. Governance is what takes sourcing maxims from words to reality, what ties together and keeps together sourcing strategies and business strategies. Good governance enables faster, better decision making.

Effective sourcing governance is crucial to Multisourcing. As is true for all forms of governance, while hard work must undeniably go into the process up front, strong sourcing governance ultimately makes every other part of Multisourcing dramatically easier and more effective.

Why You Need Strong Sourcing Governance

Why is sourcing governance so important? Most simply, the lack of governance has left many organizations with a chaotic blend of service relationships and contracts. From a positive perspective, good sourcing governance enables the enterprise not only to effectively implement Multisourcing, but also to manage the dynamic services environment that Multisourcing creates. *Effective sourcing governance is more important to long-term sourcing success than any other factor.* Governance is the foundation of sourcing agility, and sourcing agility spawns business efficiency, effectiveness, and growth. Specifically, there are five major reasons that sourcing governance is absolutely critical.

1. *Effective sourcing governance can turn disruptive and noninte-grated services into high-performance service delivery operations.* Good governance that effectively engages the consumers of services (who set demand), enterprise executives (who set the goals and rules), and providers of services (who determine how a service is delivered) creates the environment for managing

changing needs and resolving other issues—without necessarily having to go through the expensive and disruptive process of replacing providers.

2. *Good sourcing governance means better outcomes.* The goal of Multisourcing is achieving required business goals, nothing else. Good sourcing governance ensures that all sourcing actions are directed at these goals and not drawing resources (money or management focus) away from their achievement.

3. *Good sourcing governance synchronizes sourcing strategy with business strategy as business strategy changes.* An indisputable fact of modern business management is that business strategy changes far more often because the competitive and market environments change far more rapidly than in the past. A set of sourcing actions focused on achieving today's business requirements are only temporarily beneficial. Business strategy and business requirements will change, and sourcing strategy and sourcing actions must stay synchronized with these changes. Without good governance, a well-aligned sourcing strategy is simply a poorly aligned sourcing strategy waiting to happen.

4. *Good sourcing governance encourages desirable sourcing behaviors by the providers and consumers of services.* Ultimately, sourcing governance creates the environment for desirable behaviors in sourcing by all parties. Your organization and your network of service providers are partners in achieving your goals, not automatons. All the parties involved in the relationship will make sourcing decisions daily. These decisions will either support or undermine the achievement of business goals. Governance sets up the rules and the structure for good decisions to be made by all parties without the need for omnipresent oversight.

5. *Good sourcing governance is your best approach for the management of sourcing risk.* Risk is a fact of life. Organizations have to manage the risks that go along with Multisourcing. Governance helps you ensure that good management practices

are in place and will be used, therefore helping you mitigate sourcing-related risks.

How can you recognize good or poor sourcing governance when you see it? We've found a number of markers of effective sourcing governance. The first is the explicit existence of a sourcing council that is made up of the senior executives of the organization (chapter 2). When senior executives are involved at the highest level of sourcing governance, all other aspects of governance function more effectively. The major reason is that these executives understand and support (with people and economic resources) the need for sourcing governance.

Another marker of good governance is that the governance models for sourcing are stable year to year. This, of course, does not mean that governance is static, or that changes are not occurring in the provider mix, service delivery, or service requirements. It means instead that the governance processes themselves remain stable. Good governance takes time, and if the processes are changing constantly, there will inevitably be gaps and misalignment.

A third marker is that formal and well-understood processes for exceptions exist and are monitored. Not all sourcing decisions or actions will follow the enterprise rules—sometimes you will need to make decisions outside the general guidelines and approaches. Good governance recognizes this and allows for it by defining, in the enterprise context, when exceptions to the standard processes and decision criteria are allowed. As long as everyone understands when and why these exceptions are permissible, they serve to strengthen the governance process rather than undermine it.

Fourth, good sourcing governance includes formal methods of communication. We've already discussed how important communication is to sourcing actions, and we expand on this topic later. But communication is also important to sourcing governance—all the parties must understand how the governance process works, what decisions are made, and how those decisions affect them. This is impossible without formal communication processes to distribute information between service consumers, service recipients, and service providers.

Finally, good governance includes a system of controls and records. In addition to assigning decision rights and accountabilities, one of the important requirements of good governance (and one that ties governance to compliance requirements) is that it has controls to assure that governance procedures are followed and the records that prove it.

In chapters 2 and 3, we covered the first two elements of sourcing governance: sourcing maxims and sourcing initiatives. Sourcing maxims should be managed by an enterprise sourcing council that also determines the makeup of the group that sorts through sourcing choices and designs sourcing action plans. In this chapter, we'll look at the third element of sourcing governance: management. This is the largest area of sourcing governance, as it lays the ground rules for the majority of the day-to-day sourcing-related actions. Maxims should be reviewed yearly (or whenever there are significant changes in business strategy), and sourcing initiatives are typically project based; management and coordination is the everyday work of Multisourcing.

Practical Governance of Multisourcing Management

As noted, there is no prescribed governance mechanism (committee, council, office, organization chart, etc.) for Multisourcing. The correct mechanisms depend on the existing culture and processes of each organization, as well as the organization's ability to adapt and change. There are, however, very specific functions that must be performed within the domain of sourcing management. Because these functions are interdependent, we discuss them as part of an "office," the Multisourcing management office, a virtual construct that may or may not be directly reflected in an organization chart.[1]

You might think of the Multisourcing management office as performing much the same functions that central casting does for movie studios. When a producer funds the development of a project, he or she passes the script to central casting. The director of the movie informs central casting what characteristics are wanted for each character in the script. Central casting then finds actors, evaluates them against the director's and producer's needs (the director may want Mel Gibson or Tom Cruise, while the producer may want to spend less money), and recommends actors. The director and producer choose from these recommendations, and then central casting negotiates and signs the contracts. Once the movie is being made, it is central casting that approves payments to the actors according to the contract and helps resolve any contractual issues that arise. Finally, central casting receives from the producer and director feedback that influences whether a particular actor will be used again and in what type of roles or situations. Note that central casting does not set requirements but helps ensure that those requirements are met. Now, to understand the additional complications of a Multisourcing management office, imagine that many of the movies being produced changed from dramas to romantic comedies to martial-arts films during production. You can see that sound governance of sourcing management is an absolute necessity to prevent chaos in such situations.

Types of Multisourcing Management Offices

While central casting functions essentially the same way in all movie studios, there are three different governance mechanisms for implementing the Multisourcing management office that we have seen clients employ to positive effect.

1. *The true office:* Some enterprises create an actual organizational group tasked with the management and coordination of sourcing across the enterprise. The true office approach includes hiring a staff of highly experienced sourcing managers who bear responsibility for day-to-day service delivery and coordination across the enterprise. Enterprises who use the true office approach typically have appointed a chief sourcing officer to whom the Multisourcing management office reports. In some cases, this office reports to the chief operations officer or the chief financial officer. This approach works best in highly centralized organizations and is often seen in government organizations.

2. *The competency center:* The most common mechanism for implementing the functions of the Multisourcing management

office is the competency center. In this approach, a centralized organization serves an advisory and coaching role to the rest of the organization, collects and disseminates best practices, and recommends standards. Occasionally, but not often, competency centers have the authority to enforce standards. The competency center works well in enterprises that already have competency centers for other functions, or semiautonomous business units, or both.

3. *The virtual or decentralized office:* In this approach, there is high-level executive recognition of the need for Multisourcing management, and the sourcing council mandates adherence to sourcing maxims and some standards, but there is no formal organization. Each business unit takes on the governance tasks (described below) with whatever organization or personnel are appropriate to its particular situation. This approach works in highly decentralized organizations but requires an active sourcing council that ensures that each business unit is in fact performing the required governance tasks.

The Role of the Multisourcing Management Office

Multisourcing requires not only the active management of sourcing relationships but commonality in the management practices across the variety of service providers. This is the governance aspect. Thus, the role of the Multisourcing management office is twofold—determining the *standards* for management and *implementing* those standards consistently. These responsibilities boil down to three categories: service selection, service coordination, and service evaluation. Remember that at this stage, we are not talking about the actual tasks but who has the authority to define who performs these tasks and how they are performed.

Service Selection

Service selection is the process of choosing external service providers when the sourcing action plan determines that external sources are needed; governance of selection is concerned with defining the process and the participants. Most often, a committee whose required membership and approach is defined by the Multisourcing management office selects the service providers. While appropriate governance can correct for errors in service selection, a standardized process with common criteria and approaches helps the committee choose the right providers and thus makes the task of day-to-day management much easier and ensures that business service requirements are met much more quickly. Service selection involves clearly defining the needs, service levels, and scopes of work, managing the selection process, and negotiating final contracts. We address service selection more fully in the next two chapters.

Service Coordination

It is in coordination that the management of Multisourcing is truly different from the management of individual outsourcing relationships. The coordination of services, the area of governance most lacking in organizations today, involves managing three sets of relationships: between the service consumers (recall that service consumers are the business units or end users of the service) and the service providers, between the enterprise and the service providers, and between the various service providers. The goal of managing these relationships is to ensure that the needs of all parties are appropriately met—this includes the needs of the service providers, which are partners in this relationship management process. With these trilateral relationship responsibilities, you can see how important it is to establish common management approaches and processes to ensure that this work gets done effectively and efficiently. Other aspects of service coordination are the guidelines for how the organization will manage change, innovation, and delivery; the definition and clarification of requirements; process management; and communication.

An important and often overlooked responsibility of service coordination is providing early warning of change. Given its knowledge of service plans and expected outcomes, and its continuous relationships with service providers, a well-coordinated Multisourcing management office is in a unique position to detect change that may become a problem further down the road. Service coordination will then activate the various channels needed to put services back on track. This is a key function of the program governance board at Nike, discussed below.

Service Evaluation

Service evaluation encompasses measurement processes—how are service providers measured, and how is success and failure determined? Many organizations believe this element of governance begins and ends with requiring a pricing benchmark. Multisourcing requires a relationship view of your service providers, and therefore, service evaluation also requires measuring the quality of the relationship. Additionally, recognizing that the success of the entire enterprise depends on effective service sourcing, an evaluation includes the creation of multiple views of service and sourcing outcomes for multiple audiences (often displayed in a sourcing dashboard). Included on this dashboard are meaningful measures that assess the impact of service choices on business goals for the use of every level of management in the organization.

Over time, service evaluation will create a repository of the history of services in the organization, allowing the compilation of service best practices: which service providers really deliver, the best governance arrangements for each type of service, the lessons learned, and so on. That knowledge, in turn, allows the Multisourcing management office to coach service providers, driving ever-stronger relationships and performances.

Addressing the Important Issues from the Outset

For successful governance of the management of Multisourcing, these are the issues that must be addressed: selection, coordination, and evaluation. We have to emphasize again that there is no magic organizational structure for the governance of Multisourcing. Whether you decide to create a true Multisourcing management office, to have various Multisourcing management committees or communities, or to establish best-practice groups to share experiences, you will need to address these three areas.

Once you've decided what governance mechanisms you will put in place to accomplish these tasks—service selection, service coordination, and service evaluation—we can provide some specific advice for the management details that have to be accomplished within each of these tasks. For the remainder of this chapter, we'll focus specifically on the management roles and competencies of service coordination. Then we'll look at service selection in the next two chapters and service evaluation in chapter 7. Additionally we have included a look at how to measure your Multisourcing management capabilities in the appendix. Measuring your management capabilities is an important but advanced step in implementing Multisourcing. Your first focus should be on implementing your new approaches to sourcing management in support of Multisourcing.

Part II: Multisourcing Management

WHILE GOVERNANCE determines who has authority related to sourcing, management determines who has responsibility for meeting the goals and delivering value. As we've noted, Multisourcing requires new management approaches that recognize the interdependencies and fluid relationships that are created. Managing in a Multisourced environment is vastly different from managing internal service delivery. In Multisourcing, there is far greater complexity due to the number of parties involved, the interdependence of providers, and the relationships required to ensure success.

More than just managing the technical details of service delivery is required, as Nike's experience shows. "We realized that although we had a well-functioning dispute resolution process and weekly operational meetings, that wasn't enough," says Bert Liverance, director of global IT operations at Nike. "We didn't have a formal way of dealing with change, of managing risks for both sides, of working out financial issues, so that we could be proactive."[2] Working with its service provider, Nike created a program governance committee that now meets biweekly. The committee is composed of key individuals from both Nike and the service provider and includes account executives and finance and contract representatives.

Liverance notes that the meeting agenda is fluid but typically covers demand control, implementing cost-saving programs, thought leadership, and new business. "The meeting allows us to stop focusing on what's 'broken' and turn attention to how we jointly deliver value to the business. And that's the question we both [Nike's sourcing team and the outsourcer] have to be able to answer all the time: are we delivering the best service at the best cost to meet business needs; are we delivering value?"

The meetings have strengthened the relationship and improved delivery (even though there was nothing wrong when the committee was formed), according to both sides. Before the committee was implemented in 2002, there were eight outstanding contract issues. Today there are none, which Liverance attributes directly to the meetings: "The committee handles issues before they can become irritations." Nike is fully committed to this model for managing its sourcing relationships. "This model allows for periodic self-analysis, which is certainly warranted whether you outsource or not. Strong management relationships are an absolute necessity to ensure that you continue to deliver value that matters to the business."

The differences between managing Multisourcing and managing internal delivery are most evident in two areas: management competencies and roles, and management processes. Because competencies and roles bridge the gap between governance and management, we'll start there.

Multisourcing Management Roles and Competencies

Many executives we work with believe the root cause of their sourcing difficulties lies with a service provider's inability to manage service delivery well. They perceive a need to always be looking over the service provider's shoulder. This need, and the failures related to it, are in fact far more often traced to the lack of appropriate sourcing management competencies on the recipient side. The service recipients and service consumers don't retain or never had the appropriate staff to hold up their side of the bargain. A European retail chain provides an instructive example. Deciding to bring more management focus on growth, the sourcing council decided that the core finance functions would be outsourced. The internal finance staff was reduced to the CFO and a few key managers and planners. "While the relationship was a success at meeting our immediate needs at good value, we realized that we did not have the necessary internal staff and competencies to determine and set business strategy, and manage change with our provider," says the CFO of the organization. "So about a year after the contract was signed we doubled our internal staff tasked with setting strategy and standards. This new staff has been critical in helping us manage our outsourced providers and ensure our current and future needs are met." Sourcing management competencies and experience cannot be overlooked when your organization is moving to Multisourcing. As Dick LeFave, CIO at Nextel, notes, "Senior managers in a multisourced operation need to have lived the excitement of the justification phase and the anguish of the discovery of delivery challenges in the first year. They need to have done this before."[3]

What Can't Be Outsourced

As the story about the European retailer shows, certain key roles and competencies can't be outsourced. These roles have nothing to do with what services should or should not be outsourced (which we looked at in chapter 3); these roles have to remain in-house (and in some cases, this may mean new hiring because the roles did not previously exist) even when the service is outsourced. Our research and work with clients indicates that there are four such key roles (which does not mean "jobs").[4]

1. *Service leadership:* This role establishes the strategic direction of the service and delineates the business value and future needs of the enterprise in relation to this service. The service leadership role is usually filled by the lead executive for that service—the CIO, CFO, chief marketing officer, head of human resources, and so forth.

2. *Architecture and standards development:* This role oversees the levels of standardization or customization of a service over time. The goals are to ensure that future value is delivered and that outsourcing does not create process or electronic "concrete," which locks the enterprise into a single method of service delivery that can only be offered by one service provider. Architecture and standards are critical to maintaining agility and choice in service delivery over time.

3. *Business enhancement:* The business enhancement role deals with innovation and exploring ways that the service's value to the enterprise can be increased over both the short and the long term. This is particularly important for enhancement and transformation types of deals. You must have the capability to engage service providers' approaches to innovation and value critically. The myth of the steady state (discussed in the introduction) leads many organizations to overlook the importance of this role.

4. *Provider management:* Clearly, you need to invest in roles that engage with your service providers. The lack of investment in provider management is a result of the myth of self-management.

A New Set of Competencies Is Needed

Filling these roles requires competencies that may not exist within your current service delivery or service management organization. As we have discussed, current operational managers, who are most often chosen to manage external providers, are almost always the wrong choice. The cooperative management of service relationships with external providers is very different from managing internal delivery.

By working with successful Multisourcing enterprises, we've developed a general map of the competencies needed in these management roles. They fall into three categories: service-specific competencies, business competencies, and behavioral competencies (table 4-1). Obviously, service-specific competencies will vary, depending on the ser-

TABLE 4-1

Multisourcing management competencies

Service recipients will need a set of competencies to manage Multisourcing. You can draw from these competencies to create profiles for sourcing management roles.

Service specific (S)	Business (B)	Behavioral (H)
IT services:	B1 Understanding business practices and approaches	H1 Leading, inspiring, and building trust
S1 Designing technical architecture		H2 Thinking creatively and innovating
S2 Integrating systems	B2 Understanding business organization, politics, and culture	H3 Focusing on results
Finance services:		H4 Thinking strategically
S3 GAAP knowledge	B3 Behaving commercially	H5 Coaching, delegating, and developing
S4 Financial modeling	B4 Understanding and analyzing the competitive situation	
HR services:		H6 Building relationships and teamwork
S5 HRIS management	B5 Managing projects	
S6 Coaching	B6 Managing change in the business from IT applications	H7 Influencing and persuading
Marketing services:		H8 Principled negotiating
S7 Customer and market-segmentation approaches	B7 Planning, prioritizing, and administering work	H9 Resolving conflicts and other problems
S8 Competitive analysis	B8 Communicating and gathering information	H10 Being adaptable
	B9 Focusing on customers	

vice in question, but the other sets of competencies are required for all types of service management.

For each role, you can then determine what competencies are needed and the level of proficiency required in those competencies. This is called a role profile. Keep in mind that many roles may only require a basic proficiency in a particular competency. We recommend setting no more than five levels of proficiency for each of the competencies; beyond five, and the role profiles become too complex and competency measurement becomes too detailed to work in practice. These proficiency levels can be numbered or given simple labels like *novice, practitioner, advanced,* and *coach.* Figure 4-1 shows a sample role profile for provider management for call-center services that we developed in conjunction with one of our clients. The client used four

FIGURE 4-1

Role profile for provider management

The profile shows the specific competencies (keyed to table 4-1) required as well as the level of proficiency for each of the required competencies; 4 is the highest level of proficiency.

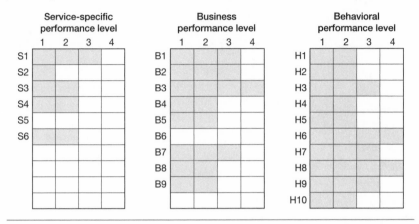

levels of proficiency, with 1 being low and 4 being high. You can map the chart to the competencies in table 4-1; the service-specific competencies were developed by the client to correspond to its call-center processes.

Alternatively, DuPont has based its approach to competencies and roles for sourcing management on the Feeny-Willcocks model, which defines nine management competencies.[5] On the basis of these competency models, DuPont has created three career paths for internal staff: business and IT vision (primary responsibility for driving growth), IT architecture (choosing, implementing, and managing standards), and service delivery (managing relationships, contracts, and measures with service providers).

One of the initial tasks of the governance of Multisourcing is the creation of these role profiles so that an organization can put in place appropriately skilled individuals. Finding personnel with the right mix of competencies should be one of your first priorities. Ideally, the competency profiles of existing staff you prepared while developing your sourcing action plans will have identified key individuals who have these competencies or show promise for developing them. If there aren't appropriate internal personnel, you'll need to hire these skills from outside—external service providers may be the first place to look. While the role of service relationship management is very different between provider and recipient, the competencies for managing relationships are similar, regardless of which side of the table you sit on. In general, external service providers have invested more in developing these competencies than have internal service delivery organizations. After all, relationship management must be a core competency for successful external providers. Don't believe that you can successfully Multisource without all of the above competencies. You will inevitably end up off course if you do not have them.

Roles, Organization Charts, and Investments

Some of the more common questions we get from clients have to do with jobs, organizational structures, and investment in Multisourcing management. While there is no one right answer to any of these questions, we can give some practical guidance. First, there are three specific jobs that many organizations create within their management organizational structure to fill the provider management role. Their applicability to any particular situation of course varies based on the number of providers being managed and the size of particular service delivery relationships.

1. *Relationship manager:* This job facilitates the development of requirements and their prioritization; manages issue escalation; monitors performance and relationships; acts as account-level liaison for the service providers and as liaison for business unit relationship managers.

2. *Performance manager:* This job is responsible for operations oversight, service integration, incidence management, and performance management.

3. *Contract manager:* The responsibilities of this job include the management of contract terms and conditions; the management

of projects and bids; and the enforcement of contracts and schedules.

At a higher level, here are some organization charts from two multi-sourced organizations in different industries, IndyMac Bank and DuPont (figures 4-2 and 4-3). IndyMac's organization chart shows its Global Resources group, which reports to an executive vice president, who is a member of the company's executive committee, and ultimately to the head of corporate development. The Global Resources group includes support for IT and business process outsourcing (BPO) arrangements, with dual reporting of relationship managers between the Global Resources organization and the business units. DuPont operates a highly multisourced IT operation; the chart shows DuPont's IT organization. All IT operations, internal and external, report through the director of what DuPont calls its Global IT Alliance. Performance managers directly oversee daily operations under the purview of a global operations manager. Relationship management and contract management functions also report to the director of the Global IT Alliance through the strategic sourcing manager.

In terms of investment in the Multisourcing management organization, figures vary widely, primarily on the basis of maturity, and are masked by incomplete accounting for costs (a topic we'll return to in a moment). Organizations new to Multisourcing should plan to spend roughly 10 percent of the value of the services you receive (across all external provider contracts and internal delivery) for effective ongoing management. However, as you master the management processes, add competency, and gain experience, you can often cut this figure to 2 or 3 percent while still performing effectively. The processes that enable this lowering of costs while maintaining effectiveness are our next topic.

Service Coordination

The core function of the management of Multisourcing is that of service coordination—this is where Multisourcing differs from simply having many outsourcing contracts. Multisourcing recognizes the interdependencies of internal and external providers and proactively manages

FIGURE 4-2

IndyMac Global Resources governance structure

There is no one right way to organize Multisourcing management, but these models from DuPont and IndyMac, two Multisourced organizations, can serve as useful templates, displaying where responsibilities lie and how they interact with each other.

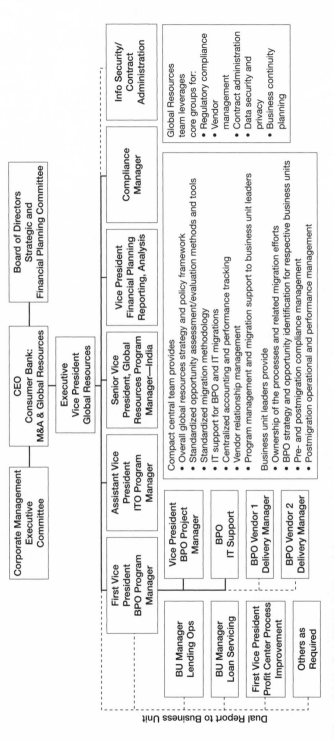

Source: IndyMac Bank FSB. Used with permission.

FIGURE 4-3

DuPont Global IT Alliance management structure

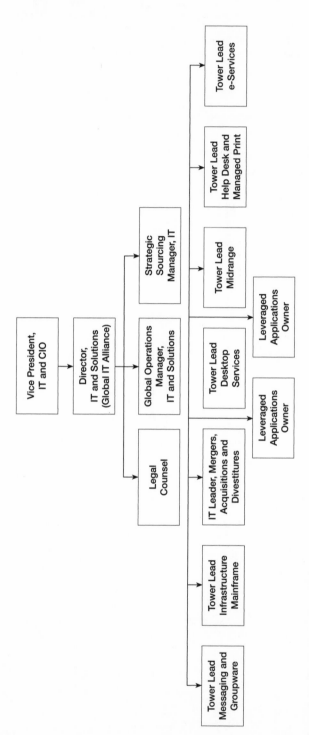

Source: E. I. du Pont de Nemours and Company. Used with permission.

those dependencies. Because this role of service coordination is so crucial to Multisourcing, we'll focus specifically on that aspect of management here. We'll cover another aspect, sourcing measurement and service evaluation, in chapter 7.

Using a balanced scorecard methodology we term the Relationship Performance Assessment or RPA (more on RPA is in chapter 7), we evaluate dozens of organizations' sourcing performance each year. Based on these evaluations, we know that nearly 50 percent of sourcing relationships are unsuccessful. The root causes of this poor performance are most often not found at the day-to-day delivery level, but in a lack of effective business-to-business management and governance at a level above day-to-day delivery. Where relationships are successful, we have found that organizations have implemented six key processes (in a wide variety of ways) to coordinate services and manage the three sets of relationships involved in Multisourcing. It is important to note that these processes need to be applied consistently for all the relationships (between consumers and providers, between the enterprise and providers, and between providers that must interface with each other) for maximum benefit. We refer to these processes as comanagement processes as they involve cooperative management between providers and recipients of services.[6]

When performed effectively, comanagement transforms sourcing deals to focus on business needs and long-term flexibility. Experience with clients has shown that organizations lacking comanagement can spend up to twice the amount managing relationships compared to those with highly effective comanagement and skilled internal teams.

Now, these cost savings may not be immediately apparent—in fact, at first glance the opposite appears to be true. Organizations not mastering these processes formally do not capture their true management costs. These management costs, though possibly hidden or disguised, are very real. They may be accounted for within other budgets, absorbed as service delivery failures, or result in costly errors due to mismatches between business requirements and delivery. No matter where they show up, they always fall to your bottom line, and therefore you can't ignore them. Organizations that do institute these processes spend much more up front, integrating these processes with their service providers and investing in properly trained and experienced personnel to manage these processes. Yet over the long haul, they save tremendous amounts in the ongoing management of their relationships and rapidly meet business needs and deliver expected outcomes.

The Six Comanagement Processes

To understand the management processes that we have found to be effective, we first need to revisit that recurrent theme: you are in a relationship with your service providers; they are neither just vendors nor the enemy. Because in a Multisourced environment you are in long-term service delivery relationships with a number of providers, you need to manage these relationships like every other relationship— together. Any amateur psychologist can tell you how a personal relationship will break down if only one party is interested in working to maintain it. The same is true in sourcing relationships—you can't do it all yourself. Successful sourcing management and coordination require a partnership with providers and consumers, all working to manage the relationship together.

There are six comanagement processes: strategy, responsibility, integration, equity, audit and assessment, and communication and feedback. These processes connect all the parties through the Multisourcing management office; they also recognize that in a Multisourced environment, there are relationships between the various providers where similar management has to occur. While each process may be implemented differently in each relationship, all the processes must be in place in each relationship for long-term success (figure 4-4). Implementing these processes means establishing roles and governance mechanisms for each of them. Implementation typically involves multiple areas of the organization, with different perspectives and interests. Not an easy task, certainly, but a crucial one.

Let's look at each of the six comanagement processes that you will engage in with service consumers and service providers.

FIGURE 4-4

The comanagement processes and the participants of Multisourcing

The six comanagement processes of strategy, responsibility, integration, equity, audit and assessment, and communication and feedback (shaded bars represent these processes) connect all the parties involved in Multisourcing.

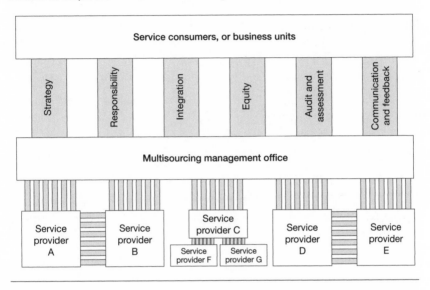

Strategy

As we've mentioned several times, it is a virtual impossibility that business strategy will not change during the course of a sourcing relationship. The comanagement of strategy navigates this change by ensuring that the parties in the relationship understand and agree on the current business strategy, the sourcing maxims, the sourcing strategy, and the delivery strategy (how services will be delivered to meet the business strategy needs). You might think of this as an understanding of the choices made in the creation of the sourcing action plans from the last chapter, and why those choices were made. Strategy comanagement is then the mechanism for communicating changes in goals, priorities, policies, and procedures as they affect the sourcing relationship. In the service consumer-to-service provider relationship, this primarily involves an understanding of, and alignment with, the changing business strategy and service needs of business units. In the enterprise-to-service provider relationship, this involves alignment with higher-level enterprise goals, and which goals have priority when there is conflict between the enterprise's and the service consumers' goals. Finally, in the provider-to-provider relationship, this process focuses on ensuring that the service providers have a common understanding of the practical impacts of strategy and any change in strategy, along with the common goals and outcomes expected from all parties. It behooves you to ensure that your service providers understand this strategy and are made aware of changes (see "Building the Comanagement Processes with Existing External Service Providers").

Responsibility

The responsibility comanagement process addresses the complex task of determining who is responsible for each of the service delivery tasks—where the lines are drawn between service consumer, the Multisourcing management office, the service provider, and other service providers that may be part of the service delivery. The responsibility process documents and defines the handoffs between each of the layers of the service's value chain when different parties are responsible for these different levels. Responsibility comanagement also clarifies the needed competencies for meeting service needs and identifies gaps in skills and competencies when needed. Thus, responsibility comanagement usually first identifies the gaps in responsibilities and capabilities between service providers and service recipients. The identification of gaps often requires a decision to move work between service providers or to add new parties to cover this gap.

Our experience with clients shows that unassigned responsibilities are one of the chief causes of service disruptions and underperformance. The management of sourcing risk in this area means paying specific attention to the handoff points between any two organizations (provider to provider, or provider to client organization). The careful and documented assignment of responsibilities is the single most effective mechanism to mitigate these sourcing risks.

BUILDING THE COMANAGEMENT PROCESSES WITH EXISTING EXTERNAL SERVICE PROVIDERS

Ideally you would design your comanagement processes before engaging a service provider, but you will also want to put comanagement in place with any existing external service providers you are using. In doing so, you will discover that many aspects of comanagement are already happening on an informal basis. Responsibility is discussed in meetings, integration in e-mails, strategy in hallway conversations.

Creating the comanagement processes in an existing relationship requires first securing the commitment of the service provider's engagement-management team to formalize and adopt these processes. Disinterest on the provider's part will be an obvious sign that there are significant problems in the relationship. In most cases, however, you will find that providers are eager to engage—comanagement benefits them by helping maintain and nurture relationships, which in turn creates opportunity for growth and ultimately should improve their long-term margins (as they are also able to reduce their spending on handling problems).

Go slowly in creating formal arrangements for each of the comanagement processes. Trying to insert too much structure into a fluid situation at one time will be counterproductive. Set quarterly milestones with a goal of finishing the design and implementation of comanagement in twelve months. Finally, be flexible—remember that this is a relationship and all relationships require give and take—and adjust your expectations where possible to effectively integrate the provider into the comanagement processes.

Integration

The comanagement process of integration handles the day-to-day interactions of service consumers and service providers. This set of codeveloped processes defines the rules of engagement between the parties involved in service delivery. It handles coordination and manages the handoffs defined in the responsibility process. You might think of the responsibility process as setting the *theory* of interaction, and integration as managing the day-to-day *implementation* of the theory—the process of ensuring that everything that needs to get done does in fact get done. Integration also identifies, creates, and documents any new procedures necessary to ensure seamless service between all parties.

Equity

The comanagement of equity is primarily concerned with value and funding mechanisms. Is the service consumer receiving value from the services provided? Are the service recipient's goals being met at a reasonable price? Is the service provider being fairly compensated for the services delivered? Are funds appropriately prioritized according to business value? Is any financial engineering in use still appropriate? It is a major requirement of Multisourcing that both the service recipient and the service provider ensure that the provider makes a reasonable profit when meeting its obligations and that the services delivered continue to provide value to the recipient. Remember that pricing is not final when a contract is signed. All along the life of the contract, the parties involved will revisit pricing, along with any changes in requirements, strategies, technology innovation, and market conditions. For example, if the market price for a service changes, the service provider will end up being paid too much or too little in comparison with the prevailing rates. If this anomaly is not addressed jointly, two problems may arise. Either the service recipient will feel cheated because it is paying too much and it may attempt to end the relationship, or the service provider will see its economic model change for the worse and will attempt to make up for lost margins by cutting corners in various ways. The equity process also ensures that the funding approach, including any financial engineering, remains appropriate for the achievement of business goals (as, for instance, cash-flow needs change).

Audit and Assessment

The comanagement of audits and assessment is concerned with verifying the facts of the relationship. What is the reported performance against service levels, and are the reports accurate? How and when is benchmarking used? Who performs the benchmarks? Are risks appropriately balanced between the recipient and the provider? The audit function is becoming increasingly important with new regulatory schemes that require additional governance controls (Sarbanes-Oxley and Basel II) and the safeguarding of customer data (HIPAA, European Union Data Protection Directive). All the parties must agree and participate in the audit process. As the name of the process implies, however, this is not just about verification of facts and documented outcomes, but also about continuous improvement based on these audited facts. All parties determine what changes would improve the audit results, where necessary. This area of comanagement is where reporting schemes and schedules are developed and implemented. All parties must decide which reports are necessary and to whom they will be directed.

Communication and Feedback

The communication and feedback comanagement process involves the transfer of information generated by all the other comanagement processes throughout the service recipient and service provider organizations so that decisions can be implemented effectively (these are internal, service-related communications, not to be confused with the communication plans that exist around sourcing strategy). A reliable reporting process and schedule must be jointly developed so that all parties are continually informed of the progress or problems relative to outcomes expected. Both parties in the relationship should also establish joint procedures for problem resolution and continuous improvement.

Key Sourcing Management Roles and the Six Comanagement Processes

The comanagement processes and the key sourcing management roles discussed earlier go hand in hand. Each of the four key roles is integral to one or more of the comanagement processes. If you don't fund these roles, you will find it nearly impossible to effectively carry out comanagement. Table 4-2 shows the relationships between the key roles and the comanagement processes.

Matching sourcing management roles and the six comanagement processes

The key sourcing management roles and the comanagement processes that each role supports.

Sourcing management role	Related comanagement processes
Service leadership	Strategy
Architecture and standards development	Responsibility, integration
Business enhancement	Audit and assessment
Provider management	Equity, responsibility, integration, audit and assessment, communication and feedback

How the Six Comanagement Processes Handle Change

It may be helpful to walk through a couple of examples of how change is managed through the six comanagement processes for a glimpse of how these processes interact and function in the real world. Let's consider two brief case studies of change in a comanaged Multisourcing environment.

Case 1: Executive Change at Service Recipient

A large manufacturing company replaced its CFO. The new CFO was focused on dramatically lowering the organization's cost of operations, which had grown rapidly during the past five years and were now significantly higher than those of competitors. The manufacturer had outsourced its entire IT infrastructure (networking, distributed computing, storage, help desk, etc.) to a prime contractor. The contract was focused on delivering best-in-class IT services and had been successful in doing so. The goals of the new CFO, however, required revising the organization's sourcing maxims and therefore a change in sourcing strategy.

Word of this change was shared through the *communication and feedback* process, and a meeting between the manufacturer's CIO and staff, the service provider's lead executives, and representatives from each of the subcontractors was called. This group was responsible for the *strategy* comanagement process, whereby the group created an understanding of the new sourcing maxims and sourcing strategy. With this understanding, the *responsibility* process was invoked, which meant a series of meetings between relationship managers to determine responsibilities for creating a plan to adjust the service levels, evaluate current projects, and look for innovation that could bring down the cost of operations. As part of the *responsibility* process, the participants decided that one of the subcontractors would be replaced by another that had more experience in managing operations to lower costs. These same relationship managers oversaw the completion of this work via *integration,* bringing all the recommendations together into a master plan. This plan was passed back to the CIO and lead provider executive for an *equity* discussion—how value and fair pricing would change on the basis of the new service levels and requirements. Finally, the *audit and assessment* process determined the new metrics that would be used to ensure that the transition to the new service levels and approaches was proceeding and to decide what new measures of success would be used in the future.

The net result was a slightly modified mix of providers, with new responsibilities, and all the providers had a clear understanding of the business goals expected. With this change, IT costs were reduced nearly 10 percent in the first six months and additional savings were realized over the next year.

Case 2: Service Provider Acquires Another Provider

A retail operation had outsourced portions of its HR function to a variety of providers. The service provider responsible for competency evaluation, training, and succession planning acquired a benefits management outsourcing firm. With the acquisition, the service provider had changed strategy and was aiming at becoming a full-service HR provider. It was thus less interested in continuing its relationships with clients for which it provided only parts of an HR outsourcing solution.

The service provider explained this change in strategy to the service recipient in a regular annual *strategy* review process. The provider informed the recipient that the change in strategy meant it would not be interested in renewing its current contract, which expired in twelve months, unless the scope of work assigned to it was increased (of course, this message was communicated with more diplomacy, but this was the bottom line!). The service recipient then employed *audit and assessment* processes and *equity* processes to gain a deeper understanding of the provider's performance and the value delivered. In this way, the recipient could determine if expanding the relationship was in its own best interests. After reviewing this data through the *strategy* process, the recipient decided that it was more comfortable in a selective outsourcing environment for HR. This decision led to ongoing efforts in the *responsibility* and *integration* processes to plan for exit from the old service provider and transition to a new one.

Implementing the Six Comanagement Processes

These examples illustrate not only the importance of the comanagement processes in accommodating change, but also how important it is to design and define at least the rudiments of Multisourcing governance and management before you begin evaluating and selecting external providers. The implementation of the six comanagement processes in your enterprise must be an important part of the requirements you set for selecting external providers. Hopefully, you can also see why governance is the single most important factor in determining the success of Multisourcing. Change is inevitable, and only enterprises that can effectively manage change in a coordinated fashion across all service providers will achieve agility and therefore competitive advantage through their sourcing actions.

In describing these cases, we were purposely vague on how each organization implemented the processes. Not only can each organization execute the processes differently, but these processes don't necessarily need to be applied in the same way in any of the relationships that must be governed and managed. You may have strategy committees to handle the strategy process with some service providers while having a dedicated relationship manager conduct the strategy process with another. However, each process has to be implemented in some way in every relationship. The appropriate implementation depends both on the respective cultures of the service recipient and the service provider and on the type of deal. In a transformation deal, for instance, the responsibility process may include a steering committee made up of service consumers, the Multisourcing management office, and a service provider. In an efficiency deal, relationship managers from each side may work out these issues. In an enhancement deal, some processes may be handled in the personal relationship between executives from the service recipient and the service provider. To avoid confusion, we should also note that each process does not imply a different staff person or committee. In fact, all the processes across several service provider relationships may be managed by the same person.

One of the most common places we see a breakdown in the six comanagement processes is when prime-contractor and best-of-breed consortia options are in use. Many service recipients fail to include all the service providers, not just the lead service provider, in their comanagement processes. They assume that the lead provider will handle those relationships. While the service recipient does not bear direct responsibility for these relationships, in the new terrain of Multisourcing, you need to actively make sure that the prime or lead service provider and the other providers are engaged in comanagement activities. In the same way that you do not ignore the actions of lower-level managers in your organization, you need to take an active role in making sure that your service providers are making effective use of comanagement. In both areas, you have to verify that managers are following through on the directives and priorities of upper-level management. You also have to implement controls to make sure that goals and priorities are communicated to all involved.

We trust that you now have a full understanding of the requirements of governing and managing Multisourcing. We cannot overemphasize the importance of sourcing governance. Through good sourcing governance, you ensure that you stay on course. It is the most overlooked and yet the most crucial part of Multisourcing success. Not until you have covered this ground will you be ready to choose providers.

Because Multisourcing is built on relationships, internal and external, you cannot expect to create the proper relationships with service providers until you deal with these issues of authority and responsibility. During the selection of service providers, you need to understand your own approach, communicate that approach to possible providers, and negotiate contracts that take your approach into account. So before evaluating and choosing service providers, you need to take the following steps:

1. Create your sourcing governance models and assign clear authority for decisions for each of the sourcing governance elements, particularly sourcing coordination.

2. Assign resources and responsibility for sourcing management.

3. Design processes appropriate to your organization's culture and management approach for ensuring that each of the six comanagement processes will be carried out.

Once you have taken these three steps, you'll be ready for the next step in the journey and where we turn in the next chapter—the implementation of your sourcing action plans by choosing providers according to the guidelines of Multisourcing governance.

CHAPTER five

Evaluate and Select
Service Providers

I F YOU PICKED UP THIS BOOK LOOKING FOR HELP IN the midst of a provider selection process and have proceeded to read the earlier four chapters, it will be very evident now why so many organizations struggle to bring ad hoc outsourcing under control. The reason is that they select providers without reference to strategy or with no formal governance or relationship-management processes in place. For many, the only time outsourcing gets sustained attention from executives is during the selection and negotiation process. Attempting to choose the best providers without a sourcing strategy or sourcing governance is like the task of Sisyphus, the mythic king condemned to eternally roll a stone up a hill, only to have it roll down again.

Back in the introduction, we discussed a number of myths related to outsourcing that were the source of many organizations' struggles. One of those myths, what we call the myth of the enemy, begins to rear its head once you've created your sourcing action plans, designed your governance models for externally provided services, and begun to evaluate possible external service providers. The myth of the enemy, as we've referenced before, is the idea that external service providers are the enemy—dishonest, untrustworthy characters, totally focused on sucking as much money as possible out of your pockets while purposefully undermining your goals. As a service recipient, you may be interested to know that the service providers have often viewed their customers as dissembling manipulators bent on hiding critical information and changing the terms of their contracts on a whim.

As we hope we have demonstrated by now, this view of outsourcing has no place in Multisourcing. In reality, both the service recipient and the service provider are simply trying to control risk and maximize options. Both providers and recipients have to move beyond the myth of the enemy and begin to craft what we call win-win-win relationships.

Why are adversarial relationships so counter to Multisourcing, and why are win-win-win deals necessary? One client that engaged us for help in quickly selecting a new service provider provides a great illustration. The client needed to find a new service provider right away because its current provider had just filed for bankruptcy and service disruptions were occurring. One of the parties involved in the new selection and negotiation was a procurement specialist from the organization's purchasing department. During the introduction, this individual boasted that she had negotiated such a "good" contract with the existing service provider that the relationship had forced the provider into bankruptcy. Despite the fact that only two years into an expected five-year relationship, the organization had to undergo the time-consuming and costly process of choosing a new provider (and that service interruptions were causing pain across the enterprise), most everyone at the organization concurred that another bankruptcy-causing contract was the ideal.

The business and competitive landscape of the near future will require organizations to depend on a network of internal and external service providers. While some relationships in this network will clearly be more important than others, no organization can afford to spend management time and business cycles on the management of disruptions in this network because of bankruptcies or failed contracts, rather than on competing. Therefore, Multisourcing requires the creation of relationships that are not only cost-efficient but also stable and flexible. You cannot afford relationships that are adversarial and liable to fail. Thus, there are three parties to any external service relationship: the external service provider, the service consumers and their business needs, and the service recipient enterprise. In other words, you need to create relationships that are profitable for your service providers, deliver the needed business outcomes for the service consumer (whether external customers or internal business units), and make financial sense for the enterprise as a whole. These are the three wins of a win-win-win deal.

Crafting such win-win-win relationships starts with your strategy and governance, but is implemented by your selection, evaluation, and negotiation processes. And most organizations employ evaluation and negotiation processes that continue to perpetuate the myth of the enemy. These enterprises are focused on negotiating a rock-bottom price at all costs, not on choosing the appropriate party with which to build an ongoing service relationship to achieve business outcomes. Increasingly, service providers also recognize the downside of entering contracts that aren't built on the right foundation. As Brian Keane, CEO of Keane, Inc., a midsized business process and IT-service provider, notes, "Real success requires a high degree of cultural compatibility between the client and the provider organization, including a shared commitment to achieving business outcomes. In our experience it's better for us to gracefully decline to bid where price is the primary decision-making criterion. Those situations typically result in missed expectations, high turnover, lost time, and poor results for both sides."[1]

Proper evaluation of service providers is an intricate exercise that is based on many factors. Governance, comanagement, and relationship factors, as we discussed in the last chapter, are of primary significance; you have to peel back the layers of the service providers to look at their competencies, aptitudes, culture, proven past performance, and business model. Although it is perhaps an overused analogy, you are entering a marriage with your service providers. Just as you wouldn't choose a spouse on the basis of only superficial qualities, you need to gain deep insight into the character of the candidates and—what is critical—

allow them to gain deep insight into yours. Relationships are not one-way affairs. Both parties must completely understand the other's goals and needs if they are to form a successful relationship. Let's look specifically at the typical service provider evaluation processes used today, examine typical errors, and then consider an effective alternative.

What's Wrong with Traditional Evaluation Processes?

WHILE WE'VE NOTED that traditional evaluation processes are not conducive to building successful win-win-win deals, we need to look deeper to understand exactly why—and then adjust the approaches for success in Multisourcing. Two common evaluation alternatives in use today are the traditional request for proposal (RFP) alternative and the sole-source alternative.

Traditional RFP Evaluations

The traditional RFP evaluation begins when the organization assembles a core team of people who are intimately familiar with the service to be outsourced as it is being performed today. This group focuses on creating a laundry list of (usually) open-ended questions covering every aspect of how a service provider operates and delivers a service. Often the group borrows pieces of other RFPs from around the company, the Internet, or vendor white papers; includes some standard financial-discovery documents required by the purchasing department; and sends this lengthy document out to every provider it can find that might provide the services it needs. Generally, this pool comprises seven to ten service providers, but often even more.

The service providers receive this document that requires perhaps hundreds of man-hours to respond to, but often they are not structured properly, and contain little information about the service recipient's true needs, executive expectations, or current environment. They make a calculated guess on their chances of winning the deal, which with so many providers competing is relatively low. Some decide not to respond at all; most others decide to put minimum effort into the response, answering questions vaguely, mostly with boilerplate marketing language borrowed from past RFP responses.

The service recipient team receives the responses and attempts to make a good decision based on the disparate responses from the service providers, many of which don't actually answer the question asked (because the questions were nonspecific and a response format was not mandated). After spending many man-hours trying to create a somewhat level comparison on the basis of the RFP responses, the service recipient chooses one to three respondents and enters negotiations.

At this stage in the process, typically three to six months have been spent and there are still months of negotiations ahead. Meanwhile, in this typical scenario, the service recipient and provider know virtually nothing about each other. The provider does not know the actual scope of work that is required, the service levels that are needed, the type of relationship expected, what other service providers it may need to work with, or the current state of the organization. The recipient knows little about the provider's business model, its delivery and relationship-management personnel, or its culture. This is hardly a recipe for future relationship success.

Sole-Source Alternative

Rather than the traditional RFP process, which approaches multiple providers, the sole-source alternative goes directly to the negotiating table with a single service provider. The sole-source approach is often a reaction to the cost and time expense of the traditional RFP approach. In some cases, it is instituted by a newly arrived executive who has been hired by the CEO or board of directors to implement change quickly. This executive does not want to spend the time necessary to run a traditional RFP process and so dictates negotiations with a single provider (although sole-source negotiations often take just as long or longer, since the recipient has no negotiating leverage). At other times, the sole-source approach is adopted because the recipient already has a relationship with a provider to deliver other services. Rather than shop around, the recipient chooses to stick to the "tried and true." A sole source also occasionally is the result of beginning an RFP process. In these cases, a service provider receives the RFP and rather than responding, uses its connections with senior executives or the board to short-circuit the process. These higher-ups issue a mandate that the RFP process be shut down and that the sourcing team move directly to negotiations with a specific provider.

While the sole-source approach often avoids the time and expense of the RFP, it presents many of the same problems, and some extra ones. Typically, in the sole-source approach, the provider and recipient still know next to nothing about each other. All of the discovery process will happen at the negotiation table. Additionally, a sole source approach takes much of the negotiating power out of the hands of the service recipient. In our benchmarks, we've found that sole-source negotiations typically result in costs 50 percent higher than market average.

The Alternative: A New Approach to the RFP Process

THERE IS an alternative approach that steers between the time and expense of traditional RFP processes and the ultimately higher costs of the sole source approach. We developed this new approach working with clients over the last decade as a viable alternative that can overcome the deficiencies of traditional alternatives.[2] We call this process *Fast Track* because it cuts through much of the time of the traditional approach to RFPs but maintains the critical parts of a proper RFP process. These critical parts include detailed statements of work, due diligence by both parties, and the necessary element of competition between providers to ensure an appropriate ultimate cost of the deal. The Fast Track process moves much of the detailed work about expectations, baselines, and service levels typically done during negotiation into the preparation phase, before providers are engaged. By doing so, this approach ensures that all parties have the information they need to make informed decisions, and sets the stage for negotiating a win-win-win deal. The Fast Track process also recommends prequalifying providers and thereby limits the number of providers you must thoroughly evaluate. Prequalifying providers requires either an existing deep knowledge of the relevant market and current external service providers or the retention of expert outside help (see "Fast Track and Government Organizations"). If you have this knowledge of a particular services market or engage the required outside help, limiting the number of competitors, and letting the providers know that there are limited number of competitors, provides a number of advantages. Each provider understands it has a much higher chance of winning the engagement. Consequently, the competing providers have incentive to invest the significant resources necessary to respond. When implemented correctly, limiting providers produces far better, more detailed responses, which are easier to evaluate and which require less clarification and negotiation.

We will explain the Fast Track process step by step, but for now will summarize it briefly. With the Fast Track approach, you will first create not a laundry list of questions, but a detailed statement of work and contract. Next, you send this statement to relevant providers (two to four providers if you have prequalified). The providers respond not with vague answers, but with a price and an approach to meet the statement of work. You then score the providers' responses and presentations on the basis of an agreed-on set of criteria, and you enter negotiations with one or two finalists with which you share a deep understanding of each other's requirements and needs. So, the Fast Track alternative employs critical parts of an RFP, but saves time and produces better results. As you can see, Fast Track requires that you have thought through the sourcing strategy and governance issues we covered earlier—without this information, you can't provide the level of detailed information to prospective providers that the Fast Track process requires.

Because the Fast Track is not widely used and therefore not widely understood, the first critical step in adopting it is governance related.

FAST TRACK AND GOVERNMENT ORGANIZATIONS

For the best results, the Fast Track process limits the number of prospective providers you will engage. This allows the service providers to commit the necessary resources to truly engage because they have a high probability of success. Most government organizations, however, are constrained by law. They cannot limit the number of participants in the same way that private organizations can.

The benefits of Fast Track, however, are not wholly dependent on limiting the participants. We have used the Fast Track process with many government clients with great success. The core benefit of Fast Track is the detailed work that goes into creating very specific requirements around your service needs and the choices that you have made about service delivery. Regardless of the number of participants, this work is necessary to create a foundation for effective service relationships that meet your needs. In fact, not only is the Fast Track appropriate even when the participants can't be limited, but it is also often used in sole-source negotiations. Again, Fast Track creates the environment for successful relationships.

You must gain the approval and endorsement for this new approach from the sourcing council, chief sourcing officer, or other sourcing governance body that your organization is using. Further, the affected business unit executives, senior executives, and the board need similar understanding and approval. Failing to have their approval invites service providers, particularly those not invited to participate or those not selected as finalists, to attempt to circumvent the process. If leading executives do not understand and approve of the Fast Track process, the likelihood that a service provider will succeed with this tactic is much greater. Finally, all members of the committee or team that will evaluate and negotiate with the service providers have to understand and agree to the process. Fast Track's full benefits are only realized if everyone involved is on the same page.

Four Phases of the Fast Track Process

Fast Track has four phases: (1) build the team that will conduct the evaluation, selection, and negotiation; (2) create the provider packet, the set of information that specifically defines exactly what you are seeking from service providers; (3) evaluate the providers on the basis of their responses, their presentations, and your due diligence; and (4) negotiate the final contract. We'll look at the first two phases in this chapter, and the final two phases in chapter 6. Again we turn here to a linear description of the Fast Track process; you will find in practice that many aspects of each phase actually happen in parallel.

The Importance of Your Communication Plan

B EFORE YOU EVEN begin the process, however, we must return to your communication plan. We discussed the importance of this plan as part of your sourcing strategy. Now that you have decided which services you will outsource, it's time to implement your communication plan. To ensure the selection of providers capable of building the right relationships with you, you must secure the extensive work and the participation of many members of your organization. If at any point you believed you could keep your plans under wraps, you will no longer be able to do so. We must reiterate that secrecy is impossible and that complete, open, and honest communication with staff is the only approach that pays off in the long run.

So what are the elements of your communication strategy? First, you need to identify the key messages regarding your decision: why a change is necessary, why the particular change was chosen, what the scope of change is, and the time frame for change. Your business and sourcing maxims are the perfect platform for communicating why a change is necessary—your message should clearly align with the maxims you have created. The documentation of your sourcing action plan provides the basis for communicating how the change decision was made as well as the scope of the change (who is affected, what services are affected, what is not affected, etc.) On the time-frame issue, you will want to communicate the expected milestones of your evaluation and negotiation processes. Update the schedule often to recognize progress or unexpected delays.

Second, you need to identify the audiences for your messages. You'll find they fall into these general categories: board of directors, executive team (including business unit managers), service consumers (the staff that consume the services or the services' output), current service providers (the staff, whether internal or external, that currently provide the service), customers, stockholders, and the press. For the individuals in each of these categories, you need to identify how the change will affect them and their level of knowledge and interest regarding the specific service under consideration.

With this audience segmentation, you can design your messages appropriately to ensure that the audience receives the information that it most cares about. However, you also need to consider what communication practices will be most effective by audience type. While you may use press releases to communicate with shareholders and the national or international press, you may use other methods for other audiences. You may find that interviews work best for communicating with the local press and that "town halls," similar to the companywide conference call IndyMac used to communicate its offshoring plans, work for current service (internal or external) providers. You may use the corporate intranet to communicate with service consumers. Keep in mind that supervisors and managers need special attention and access to information. The more employees hear, "I don't know," from their direct management, the faster morale will plummet and the faster your best personnel will walk out the door. Again, though, the choices in your communication strategy all depend on the level of change expected from the audiences and their level of knowledge and interest in the service.

Finally, you need to ensure that there are feedback mechanisms so that you can confirm that the messages you are trying to communicate are being heard, understood, and internalized. These feedback mechanisms may also illuminate additional messages that you need to distribute to clear up points of confusion. While you might find an e-mail inbox for questions and comments necessary, there is no substitute for what spy agencies like the CIA call *human intelligence*. Your feedback process needs to include managers and other staff who are part of each audience and who can help you gauge how their peers are responding to the messages. Human intelligence is also vital to keeping you informed about morale and rumors that may impede your plans.

Some organizations also have strong and influential employee unions. You will certainly need a specific communication plan for union employees and may even want to engage union representatives in the creation of sourcing action plans.

The key message here is to communicate early, communicate often, and communicate consistently.

Fast Track Phase One: Build the Evaluation Team

THE FIRST STEP in the Fast Track process is to create the evaluation team according to the guidelines set by your sourcing governance. The evaluation team will carry the process through to completion, but not all members of the team will participate in every part of the process. The team oversees the entire evaluation, selection, and negotiation process; assigns tasks to various groups; integrates their output; and ensures compliance with the guidelines laid out by the enterprise sourcing governance construct (sourcing council, chief sourcing officer, etc.). At a minimum, the team needs to include the following members:

- A project manager

- A representative from each affected business unit

- A current service expert

- The relationship manager who will be the primary point of contact with the future service provider

- Representatives covering the six comanagement processes according to how you have designed them

- A negotiation expert

- A contract and legal expert

Of course, the number and experience of these individuals should be appropriate to the size of the deal in question. Depending on your experience, you may also want to include external advisers as part of your team. Keep in mind as you enter this process that the majority of people on your team will be working on one sourcing decision a year. The personnel from the service providers will most likely have worked on hundreds if not thousands of contracts. There will certainly be an experience mismatch, which can be a significant impediment to achieving your goals. Adding expertise to your team in the form of consultants can go a long way in leveling the playing field. Given that many organizations now portray themselves as experts in outsourcing, your team will have to do some due diligence before bringing in additional help. Ensure that the consultants you engage have worked on projects with similar service needs; types of deals (efficiency, enhancement, transformation); contract or enterprise size; industries; and geographies. In addition, of course, make sure that they have referenceable accounts that have enjoyed not just low prices but a positive multiyear relationship.

Before moving on to phase two of the Fast Track, the evaluation team needs to accomplish two tasks. First, it must gather the inputs needed for the process and make sure they are up-to-date. Then it must specify the interaction plan.

Gather and Update Inputs

Before you begin the Fast Track process, you will need to gather all your decision inputs—the information used and the decisions involved in the formation of your sourcing action plan. This input includes your business strategies, business maxims, sourcing maxims, IT and other service-line maxims if you've created those, service baselines, choices of deal types, levels of customization and sourcing models, and so on. If more than two months have passed since the information was gathered and those choices were made, or if there have been material changes in the business environment (new executives, mergers and acquisitions, new competitors, change in regulations, etc.), you'll need to review the information and choices with your evaluation team to make sure that they are up-to-date.

Specify Your Interaction Plan

The next task for your evaluation team will be to agree on an interaction plan. This plan lays out everything about how you will interact with the service providers you are evaluating. It is crucial to agree on the interaction plan, as it builds the foundation for the relationship you will ultimately have with your service provider. If members of your evaluation team circumvent the rules of interaction, you can be sure they will circumvent the governance and relationship-management processes you will put in place with the selected service provider.

The interaction plan needs to specify numerous details:

- Who will be the points of contact for the evaluation team (the project manager, the relationship manager, etc.)

- How will information be exchanged with providers (e-mail, phone, fax, written documents)

- The schedule of interaction (when the provider packet will go out, when responses are due, when oral presentations will be made, when a final selection will occur)

- How many providers will receive the packet (between two and four)

It is also crucial to specify at this stage how providers that attempt to circumvent the interaction plan will be dealt with. You can be sure that, deliberately or accidentally, a service provider will call the wrong person while trying to get information or will test the waters with senior executives. Keep in mind that these actions reveal the character of the service providers you are evaluating. It is the first test of trust in the relationship—a provider that tries to go above the heads of the selection committee will go above the heads of the relationship manager and other governance personnel once a deal is signed. So, in this interaction plan, you need to explain to the providers the consequences of not adhering to the interaction plan. Don't make empty threats—ensure that you can enforce the consequences that you lay out. If senior executives balk at giving the evaluation team the authority to enforce consequences, you need to revisit your governance plan. Clearly, executives are not comfortable delegating authority to the selection process you have created.

Fast Track Phase Two: Create Your Provider Packet

THE NEXT PHASE of the Fast Track process is to create the provider packet, the complete set of information that the service providers will need to understand your goals, expectations, and requirements. This is the foundation of building a successful relationship— you cannot build on an incomplete foundation if vital information is hidden, misrepresented, or confusing. Many clients find this part of the process a bit frightening because it requires revealing more information about themselves than they are used to. The provider packet, however, is a critical success factor for sourcing services rather than tangible goods. You are building an ongoing multiyear relationship that must be founded on trust, and trust develops from disclosure and verification.

The provider packet consists of seven elements that we'll discuss in detail:

1. Enterprise objectives

2. General contract terms and conditions

3. Services statement of work (SoW)

4. Governance SoW

5. Human resources SoW

6. Pricing

7. Exit plan

These elements are actually the contract you will ultimately sign, once specific items are negotiated, with a chosen provider. This is the essence of the Fast Track process—the evaluation process is centered around the actual contract document rather than leaving specifics to the negotiating table. This level of information and specificity allows the providers to gauge their chances of winning and therefore commit the resources necessary to provide a response that is targeted to your needs and clearly comparable to other providers' responses.

Enterprise Objectives

The first part of your provider packet is a statement of your enterprise objectives in general and for this service specifically. This is mostly a high-level view that explains why you are looking for a service provider (reduced costs, better service, increased agility, competitive differentiation, etc.). The enterprise objectives should probably be based on your business and sourcing maxims. The amount of information you provide here will be dependent on the deal type. In an efficiency deal, this set of information can remain cursory and limited to the service in question. In a transformation deal, however, information about business strategy, sourcing maxims, competitors, and so forth, will be crucial to the service providers' ability to propose solutions that truly meet your needs. Remember, when you are contracting for enhancement and transformation deals, you are doing so because you expect the service provider to bring true innovation and best-in-class process knowledge and capability. By providing this insight into your business and goals, you are giving the providers the opportunity to display these capabilities in their responses.

General Contract Terms and Conditions

The first contractual elements of your provider packet are the general terms and conditions. The general terms and conditions should follow the standard templates your organization uses for contracts. However, you will need to validate that the boilerplate terms and conditions are valid for the service under consideration. For instance, while boilerplate contracts should include clauses covering confidentiality and regulatory compliance, if the service provider will have access to confidential customer information or sensitive financial information, these issues will need to be covered in the service level agreements in the services statement of work, not by boilerplate contract language. There are a number of topics that should be covered in the general terms and conditions:

- Warranties, liabilities, indemnifications, and insurance

- Payment terms, invoicing, etc. (not pricing)

- Security, confidentiality, and intellectual-property ownership and protection

- Data ownership

- Governing jurisdiction

- Regulatory compliance requirements

- Term and termination clauses

- Record keeping and audit rights

Don't gloss over these terms and conditions—make sure you know what is in them. We participated in a relationship assessment at a company we'll call Services Inc., where the relationship had soured because of a minor issue covered in the basic terms and conditions. Services Inc.'s contract incorporated many best-practice elements. There was, however, a lack of clear communication and process around invoicing. For a variety of reasons, about a year into a multiyear contract, the provider began missing service levels. The contract called for the provider's fees to be reduced by a specific percentage that was based on these failures; all parties agreed on the amount of the fee reduction. However, the provider submitted full-price invoices, believing that Services Inc. would deduct the required amount before paying. Services

Inc. assumed that the provider would deduct the specified fee reductions before submitting the invoice. No one communicated to Services Inc.'s finance department what the correct payment amount was, and so the invoices were paid at full price. This mistake was not discovered until a six-month audit was performed—and immediately, suspicion flared. The lesson: all contract details are important.

Services Statement of Work

Your services statement of work is the detailed set of requirements for the services under consideration. The services SoW contains seven elements: scope, roles and responsibilities, service levels, measurement, incentives and fee reductions, transition, and innovation.[3]

Scope

The scope section of the SoW defines the services that you are seeking and must contain the business outcomes you delineated when you began to develop your sourcing action plan. Additionally, it contains the detailed baseline information that you gathered while evaluating your current competency in delivering the service. The service providers must have this detailed information to understand the current situation and how it may need to change and hence to provide accurate bids. This is where you will detail the level of customization you require on the basis of your "four worlds" choices—what elements of service can be standardized and what elements must conform to your existing processes, IT architecture, and culture.

Finally, the scope section needs to detail any material projects that are currently under way and that will change the baseline, and your expectations for how the service provider will adapt, take over, or handle the transition of these projects. We have seen countless relationships thrown off the rails at the very outset because projects in progress were not included in the baseline.

Roles and Responsibilities

It is essential that the SoW contain a detailed description of the roles and responsibilities for each service. Having these roles and responsibilities fully defined avoids issues of finger pointing and confusion about which party is responsible and who should be performing various functions. The discussion of roles and responsibilities should focus particularly on the transition process, as this is a common stumbling block at the beginning of service relationships. The goal is formal agreement on which party will own each of the major aspects of service delivery and service management.

Service Levels

The next critical portions of your services SoW are the service level agreements (SLAs) around service delivery. An SLA is a framework that sets service provider and recipient expectations. It describes the services to be delivered; identifies mutual responsibilities; specifies the metrics by which the effectiveness of service activities, functions, and processes will be measured, examined, and controlled; and delineates any penalties or incentives related to those metrics.

The development of these SLAs is the major task in preparing your services SoW. The evaluation team may take this task on as a group or assign it to a set of service experts. Developing good SLAs requires experience. Many of your internal functions may be run using SLAs today—you should tap some of the experience inside your enterprise to assist with SLA development. Many SLA templates related to efficiency deals are also available from a variety of sources, in print and online. The templates are not useful for enhancement or transformation deals, however, as these need to be so highly specific to your organization's current state and future needs.

In SLA development, you will need to uncover a layer beneath the business objectives that you have already identified. Your SLAs need to be more specific about the outcomes and the pieces that go into achieving these outcomes. To uncover this layer, your SLA development team will most likely want to spend time interviewing current service providers and service consumers.

In general, a good SLA covers such specific details as the availability of service, response times, joint responsibilities, escalation processes, and defined quality measures in terms of business outcomes. The greatest danger in SLA development is to revert to the habit of specifying *how* service is delivered rather than focusing on outcomes.

You should keep in mind some other factors when developing SLAs:

- *Geography:* Will the service metrics be the same worldwide, or are there variances by geography?

- *Needs:* Do all consumers of the service require the same service levels, or are there distinct groups that require higher levels or can tolerate lower levels of service?

- *Dependency:* Do certain service levels depend on other service levels being met? Will the service provider's ability to meet a service level depend on the performance of another external or internal service provider?

- *Measurement and perception:* Are the service levels objectively and consistently measurable? Do the perceptions of the service consumer match these objectively measurable service levels?

- *Management:* Do you have the capability and retained staff to effectively monitor and manage the SLAs you are creating?

We can use the business outcomes we specified during the development of the sourcing action plan to illustrate the creation of service levels. Table 5-1 compares the level of detail necessary both in business-outcome statements and in service level statements.

Measurement

The measurement section of the services SoW defines how the achievement of SLAs will be measured and audited. This should be based on the audit and assessment comanagement process you defined in chapter 4. It is critical that you and the provider agree on how data will be collected and evaluated, as disagreement about this is the easiest way for relationships to break down from the outset. Your measurement section may specify the use of third parties to help create and audit the measures.

TABLE 5-1

A comparison of statements of business outcome and statements of service level

Business outcome	Service level
Pay all employees in the U.S., Canada, and the U.K. accurately, following all applicable reporting and tax regulations.	Pay 12,000 employees in the U.S., 1,000 in Canada, and 3,000 in the U.K. accurately, following all applicable reporting and tax regulations, 24 times per year.
Provide three qualified interview candidates for each opening.	Provide three qualified interview candidates for each opening within three weeks.
Process invoices within 72 hours of receipt.	Process 80 percent of invoices within 72 hours of receipt.
Provide end-to-end uptime (PC, applications, network connectivity) to all users.	Provide 90 percent end-to-end uptime (PC, applications, network connectivity) to 3,000 users in two locations.
Provide adequate bandwidth to all locations, with no significant downtime.	Provide 2 terabytes of bandwidth, with 99.7 percent availability.
Resolve user problems expediently and with high-quality customer service.	Resolve 67 percent of trouble tickets on the first call; direct 98 percent of escalation requests to the correct queue.
Answer customer calls quickly, and raise levels of customer satisfaction.	Answer 100 percent of calls before third ring; hold times will not exceed three minutes.

This section should always include a benchmarking clause that states that you can use external benchmarking services to verify measurement and to compare service levels and costs to external figures. You might never invoke this clause, but it needs to be included for risk-mitigation purposes.

Incentives and Fee Reductions

The section on incentives and fee reductions goes hand in hand with the SLA section and provides a link to the pricing section that we'll address shortly. Many use the term *penalties* instead of *fee reductions*. Penalties, however, are generally disallowed by contract law (although this varies by country), while fee reductions are generally enforceable. Hence we use the term *fee reductions*. In this section, you need to specify whether there are service level targets whose achievement will produce higher fees and the fee reductions associated with failure to meet targets.

When creating incentives and fee reductions, you need to tie them to the business impact of achieving, or failing to achieve, service levels. Often, organizations offer incentives that reward providers for achieving service levels that add little or no value to the recipient. Similarly, many organizations fail to tie appropriate fee reductions to harm. A simple example helps illustrate how incentives and fee reductions should be created.

Imagine a manufacturing line that produces 500 widgets a day. A service provider is responsible for ensuring that the IT infrastructure supports the manufacturing line—the production of 500 widgets a day requires a service level of 99 percent availability for the IT infrastructure. The service provider charges $500 for achieving this service level. Thus, the cost per widget of achieving this service level is $1. An incentive should only be created if exceeding 99 percent availability provides the capability of producing additional widgets. If 99.5 percent availability would allow the production of 510 widgets per day, then there is business value in the overachievement and the cost per widget of the service decreases. An incentive can be created that rewards the service provider—but only up to a portion of the business benefit received. The incentive should not exceed $10, as this would push the cost per widget back to $1. A penalty should reflect the same approach. If 98 percent availability only allows the production of 490 widgets, fees should be reduced to a level that, *at minimum*, reduces the $1-per-widget ratio.

As a rule of thumb, fee reductions should be between 10 percent and 20 percent of fees associated with the service level. Reductions of less than 10 percent are typically not significant enough to drive provider behavior; reductions of more than 20 percent tend to drive providers toward extreme cost-cutting rather than toward improved performance.

Transition

The transition section of the SoW defines the process for moving the service from its current delivery to the service provider. This includes alternative service levels or different measures to be met during the transition process, the transition time frame, and the transition responsibilities.

Innovation

One of the greatest sources of dissatisfaction in outsourcing relationships revolves around innovation, or the lack thereof. No business executive would tolerate an internally delivered service in which costs and service levels are unchanged. Every part of a business is expected to improve by driving costs down or improving productivity or efficiency in some way. We're all expected to become better at our jobs, year over year. Few outsourcing contracts anticipate improvement in performance when requirements are steady, and even fewer take into account changing requirements. This is one aspect of the steady-state myth that we discussed in the introduction.

Your services SoW needs to consider what types of innovation and change are expected and your expectations for the role that the service provider will play in adapting to innovation, or producing innovation, in service delivery. This is especially important in enhancement and transformation deals, in which the recipient expects that significant innovation will be delivered and for that innovation to eventually become part of the baseline and be incrementally improved from there on an ongoing basis.

The innovation section of the services SoW should delineate the process for suggesting and approving innovation. This section should also specify the incentives for the provider to employ innovative approaches to service delivery. (Again, the incentives are appropriate as long as the innovation delivers business value and the provider receives a portion—not all—of that value.) We also recommend having innovation workshops during the oral presentation process—we'll discuss those in the next chapter.

Governance Statement of Work

Your governance statement of work needs to refer back to your own governance structure and the six comanagement processes defined in chapter 4. Remember, the explicit implementation will vary with your chosen deal type and the relationship model you chose when developing your sourcing action plan. The deal type helps define the sort of relationship you needed to meet business outcomes. Transformation deals require close working relationships based on trust and a deep understanding of your business model, industry, and competitive position. Efficiency deals, on the other hand, don't require relationship managers with such business acumen on the service provider's side. Your governance plan should make explicit your expectations of the competencies and the experience of the relationship manager who will be assigned to you.

Similarly, the tiers within the services value chain and the relationship model you chose will define the interaction points between the service provider for this service and other internal and external service providers. For instance, if the service under consideration is at the lowest tier of the services value chain (infrastructure), then the service provider will only need to interface with the provider of the application layer. If, on the other hand, you are contracting for business solution services under a prime-contractor relationship, the service provider will have to interface with a wide variety of other service providers, both internal and external.

Your governance SoW needs to define where the service provider fits with others and how those relationships will be governed. Of course, this statement also needs to define your deal-governance structure that the provider will be expected to interact with and adhere to. Make sure that you are explicit about how you expect disputes to be resolved—a process that you have defined in your governance mechanisms.

Human Resources Statement of Work

Your human resources statement of work needs to define explicitly your expectations for the impact of your service choices on your internal personnel and the role the service provider will play. For instance, you need to define whether you expect the service provider to take on any of your internal staff (often referred to as "rebadging"), and if so, how many. Here is where your personnel competency inventories are most needed. From those inventories, personnel reviews, and manager input, you'll need to make some decisions about key staff. You must decide which staff need to be retained to serve as advisers to your relationship manager and governance processes, and which you want to retain to manage the transition. You will want the service provider to take on other key staff and assign them to your relationship. Others can be hired at the service provider's discretion, and still others may be provided severance packages. Many organizations shy away from putting these important decisions on paper, fearful of the message they send to staff. As a result, one of the most important factors in the success of the relationship is ignored or shrouded in mystery. Remember that your staff, if not through your communication plan then through informal channels, will know at least the rough outlines of your sourcing action plan and will come to their own conclusions through a mix of rumor and hearsay. Far better that you bite the bullet and provide the information your future service provider will need to craft a successful relationship than you avoid this issue and harm your existing staff and jeopardize the future success of your sourcing arrangements.

The human resources SoW needs to cover a multitude of important issues:

- The rules of engagement that the service provider must follow to interview and select among your current staff

- The rules for compensation and benefits that will be provided to staff members who are taken on

- Any rules about how long those employees have to be retained by the service provider

- Which staff and roles you expect to retain

- Which employees you will prohibit the service provider from hiring

- An expected transition plan for employees from one employer to the other (and provision for moving staff back inside, which often occurs)

Pricing

In the pricing section of your provider packet, you are not telling the providers what their pricing should be, but laying out the pricing framework that you will use. There are five basic pricing frameworks (but each has a number of variations). Each has different risk profiles for the service recipient and the service provider and is appropriate for different types of deals (table 5-2).

- *Cost-plus pricing* is a framework in which the service recipient pays for services at the provider's cost plus a set percentage. Providers face very low risk, as their cost recovery is guaranteed; the recipient faces medium risk, as service levels may not be guaranteed. Cost-plus pricing is only appropriate for efficiency deals.

- *Fee-for-service pricing* is a variable framework based on the amount or quality, or both aspects, of the service actually delivered. There is medium risk for both provider and recipient. The providers' costs are not covered unless service levels are met; the recipient bears some risk, as costs are not entirely predictable and service levels may not be achieved. Fee-for-service pricing is appropriate for efficiency and enhancement deals.

TABLE 5-2

Matching pricing frameworks, deal types, and risk

Each of the five major pricing frameworks balances risk between recipient and provider differently and therefore is appropriate only to certain deal types.

Pricing framework	Deal type			Recipient risk	Provider risk
	Efficiency	*Enhance*	*Transform*		
Cost plus	X			Medium	Low
Fee for service	X	X		Medium	Medium
Fixed price	X			Low	High
Shared risk/reward		X	X	High	High
Business outcome achievement			X	Medium	High

- *Fixed price* sets a specific service level and a set price for delivering to that service level (no higher or lower). This is high risk for the provider, as the provider must meet the service level no matter how many resources are required. The recipient has low risk, as costs are capped, but the recipient receives no cost reduction if demand for services or service levels decreases. Fixed price is appropriate for efficiency deals.

- *Shared-risk/reward pricing* involves a flat rate with additional payments based on achieving specified outcomes. This pricing framework is appropriate for enhancement and transformation deals.

- *Business outcome achievement* is a framework in which the provider does not receive any payment unless specified business outcomes are achieved. Clearly this is high risk for the provider, but also medium risk for the recipient, as there are no guarantees that expected outcomes will be achieved. Business outcome achievement is only appropriate for transformation deals.

Keep in mind as you choose pricing frameworks that price is a factor of risk assumption. Where the provider's risk is lower, prices should be accordingly lower. Where the provider's risk is higher, expect prices for achievement to be higher.

Exit Plan

The final part of the provider packet needs to recognize that like death and taxes, the end of the relationship is inevitable. Your contract with this service provider will end either because the term is up or because other reasons have caused one party to invoke the termination clauses. Therefore, you need to plan now for the process of renegotiation or disentanglement if you decide to move the service to a different service provider. Nothing of course precludes you from renewing contracts with existing providers and enjoying successful relationships for more than a decade, such as General Dynamics and Qualex have done. When in the selection process, however, you cannot assume that such will be the case, and you can't risk the disruptions from disentanglement if it is not specified in the contract from the beginning.

Consider that you will be moving to another service provider after the current one has performed the service for multiple years. In forming the exit plan, you need to think ahead about what your organization will require to maintain service levels and to make a smooth transition to the next provider. You also need to plan for the possibility that you will move some services from one provider to another while maintaining others with the same service provider. Such situations will require a delicate touch if you want to make sure the continuing relationship doesn't suffer. Document what actions are required of the service provider during these transitions. This should include process documentation, access to historical data and baselines, key personnel (described by role) you will have the option of hiring, knowledge transfer, and so on.

With all these elements created, you have completed your provider packet and are now ready to engage possible providers. That's the topic of the next chapter.

Negotiate Your Contract

WE HAVE ALREADY LOOKED AT THE DEFICIENCIES of some provider-evaluation processes such as traditional RFPs and sole-source negotiations. The Fast Track process allows you to maintain a competitive bidding environment while you build a solid foundation for your relationship with the service provider—and save time in evaluation and negotiation. In this chapter, we'll look at the latter half of the Fast Track, where you engage potential service providers, evaluate their capabilities to meet your needs, and negotiate a contract.[1]

Fast Track Phase Three: Selection

THE THIRD SET of Fast Track activities is focused on choosing the service provider or providers with which you will enter final negotiations and ultimately form your service relationship. The activities involve choosing which service providers you will invite to participate in the Fast Track process, creating your evaluation model and scoring the provider responses, conducting oral interviews, and conducting innovation workshops.

Choosing Service Providers to Participate

Once again, you'll turn to your documented sourcing action plan for guidance on which service providers you want to include in the Fast Track process. The selection must be dictated by other choices you've already made: the type of deal, the level of customization, and the relationship model. Of course, you'll want to choose providers that have successful experience delivering services in similar circumstances. Discovering which providers have this experience requires doing some homework.

First, you'll need to investigate and understand the various providers' business models. This step corresponds to our earlier discussion of the trends in the services marketplace. Providers are moving toward more standardized services, although different providers are aiming for different landing points on the customization-versus-standardization scale. Some providers are aiming to provide only standardized services; others want to add small pieces of customization around a standardized core; still others aim to provide management standardization while charging premium prices to deliver customization. The best place to find this information for publicly held companies is in the statements to shareholders and analysts. These statements accompany the firms' quarterly and annual reports. In the United States, Regulation Fair Disclosure, or Reg. FD, requires that all public companies provide access to executive conference calls and presentations well after they are made. Examine these presentations, particularly as they discuss specific strategies for achieving predictable revenue and increased margins, for clues as to where the provider wants to be.

Your provider's future plans must be considered carefully, as you are entering a multiyear relationship in which considerable change will occur, both in your business and in the market. Will your provider support your business vision? Do your sourcing maxims set forth a competitive goal (for example, of "bleeding edge" or "leading edge") that your provider can sustain? You don't want a relationship that the provider will perceive as an impediment to its long-term goals. Will the provider be interested in providing the options and flexibility you need in the future? On the other hand, you also need to know what the providers are currently delivering. Providers that have traditionally focused on customized services, while attempting to standardize, may not have the experience in creating, managing, and maintaining standardized offerings. You're looking for a provider that has experience in delivering similar services in similar circumstances today and whose future vision matches your own plans for the service in question.

If provision of services nondomestically is part of your sourcing action plan, you'll want to filter providers on the basis of their global delivery capabilities. Some providers are limited in the geographical areas from which they can draw resources; others have personnel in every conceivable spot around the world. Examine your decisions about the location dependency of the service—must it be delivered from a particular location, or can it be delivered from any low-wage country or any country that has the necessary competencies? Geography may also be a significant factor if you are looking for standardized service delivery on-site in many locations around the globe. Relatively few providers have the global reach to deliver on-site services worldwide. These factors may limit the numbers of providers under consideration.

If you are looking for an enhancement or a transformation deal, you will want to consider experience and track record within your industry. This experience could turn in either direction: you may want to avoid providers that have done, or are doing, business with competitors, or you may only want to consider providers with deep industry knowledge.

Another consideration is relative scale. On the strength of your business case, assess the size of your deal in monetary terms and compare it to typical deals that the service provider is currently engaged in. While bigger providers may have more resources and more brand cachet, your relationship may be too small to catch their attention. On the other hand, you may be uncomfortable being the biggest fish in a small pond.

All these factors, considered at a high level, can help you filter through the universe of providers and choose which will receive your packet. Selecting providers to compete in the Fast Track process is a specific area in which outside advisers can help guide you. Reputable advisers with extensive experience in outsourcing can help you quickly identify the appropriate candidates on the basis of these criteria.

One final note on selecting providers for the Fast Track process. We seldom find that there are only one or two providers capable of providing the necessary services. Usually, myriad providers might serve. In these cases, we often encounter some angst from the evaluation team on narrowing the list to the "right" set of providers. This worry, however, belies many of the real issues at stake. Outsourcing deals rarely fail because alternative service providers are *incrementally* better at providing the service in question; they fail because the relationship is flawed. This does not mean that you can ignore capability or the fact that delivery failure is a significant cause of relationship problems, but simply that marginal differences in performance between providers are rarely the issue. Look back at the failure myths that we discussed in the introduction—none of them relates to service provider capability. The root causes of failure have to do with the relationship: the deal type is inappropriate, the governance scheme is inadequate, change is not planned for, relationship management is poor, the expected business outcomes are not shared or understood.

The Fast Track process addresses these root causes of failure by delineating exactly what kind of relationship is desired and what the goals of the relationship are. If the relationship is structured correctly, then many providers can succeed—in some sense it matters little which is chosen if the relationship is structured correctly. The incremental differences in technical competencies are usually insignificant. On occasion, only one provider has the requisite process or industry knowledge, but these are relatively rare circumstances. When they occur, it will be obvious and the question of which providers to engage will be moot. So, we advise clients, don't agonize over picking the right two to four; the proper relationship will make the chosen provider the right provider. This leads directly to the next activity of Fast Track: evaluating providers.

Before we discuss that, however, a note about process. When you send the provider packet to your chosen providers, make sure that you are also clear on the interaction plan and the rules for responding. Your interaction plan should specify the clarification process—how providers can ask questions about material in the packet if it is unclear—and the due date for the written responses. We recommend that you schedule face-to-face interactions between the internal leads of each of the services in the contract and the potential service providers so that they can clarify baselines, service level requirements, and any other information necessary to respond to the provider packet. The packet should also provide an expected date range for the oral presentations that will follow the written responses. The Fast Track process, by creating the expected contract for your relationship, also provides the framework for the providers' responses. Providers should respond to the packet by accepting, modifying, or rejecting each point of the terms and conditions, statements of work, pricing schedule, and exit plan. Additionally, of course, the providers should submit a pricing scheme for meeting your requirements.

Create an Evaluation Model and Scoring System

The next activity is to determine how the providers' responses will be evaluated. Typically, the most difficult part of this process is getting the evaluation team to agree on the significant criteria and their relative importance, given the team's different perspectives. The Fast Track process smooths this effort significantly, since it clearly defines the requirements and therefore limits the providers' responses to acceptance, modification, or rejection of your proposed contract terms. Thus, a great deal, but not all, of the subjectivity of scoring is removed. However, this doesn't remove the necessity of determining the groupings and weightings of criteria for evaluation. We have found that the most effective way of bringing a varied group with different perspectives to agreement is to create a criterion hierarchy based on the analytical hierarchy process (AHP), a well-known mathematical framework for choosing among alternatives. The AHP groups criteria together into like categories, then creates subcategories of criteria, down to the needed level of specificity. It creates a model that looks much like an organization chart. Then the criteria at each level of the model are weighted against each other. Figure 6-1 provides a sample AHP for an HR outsourcing selection.

The actual criteria, of course, will vary dramatically on the basis of what type of services are being sourced and your sourcing action plan for each service. In general, we recommend that your set of criteria include four groupings:

1. *Service delivery and service level:* Within this grouping fall all the criteria related to pricing and the actual delivery of services. We've noted before that you shouldn't specify how services are delivered but should focus on service outcomes. During the evaluation process, however, you do need to understand how the service provider plans to deliver the specified outcomes and meet your service levels. You must then assess the likelihood that the provider's plan is feasible. Always be on your guard, though, that you don't assess feasibility only on the basis of how similar their methods and processes are to your own. Of course, you'll also assess the provider's willingness and ability to meet your service levels.

2. *Contract and relationship management:* Under this grouping fall all the criteria related to contract and relationship management. Here, you will assess factors such as the experience and credibility of the proposed relationship manager, the service provider's willingness and ability to engage your defined governance processes, and the provider's adherence to your required terms and conditions.

3. *Alignment and vision:* Under this grouping fall assessments of cultural fit, innovation, and intangibles like "Does the service provider 'get it'?" This grouping may sound soft, but when building a relationship, you will probably need a provider that truly understands you and your business needs. One client we worked with hit a dead end trying to choose between two

FIGURE 6-1

A sample AHP for HR outsourcing

The AHP approach creates an evaluation model by grouping criteria and then organizing them hierarchically. The figure shows a sample hierarchy of high-level criteria for an HR outsourcing decision.

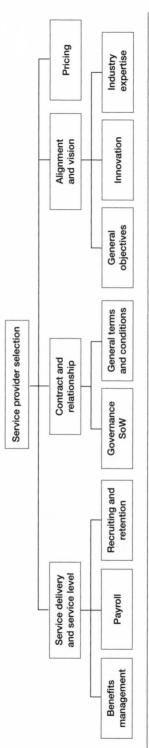

potential providers, both of which offered similar pricing, service levels, competence, and capabilities. We suggested that the client take on a project with the two providers' relationship management teams. The client chose to spend a day working on a local Habitat for Humanity project with each team. Within two hours, the client had identified which provider fit better with its team.

4. *Pricing:* Within this category fall criteria that evaluate the provider's pricing and adherence to the proposed pricing structure—and any financial engineering options that you may proactively seek. Additionally, consider any differentiation in costs related to the transition between providers.

Each of these groups of criteria have to be weighted in relation to each other. While these criteria will again vary from deal to deal and service to service, there are some general guidelines based on the type of deal you are seeking: efficiency, enhancement, or transformation (figure 6-2).

FIGURE 6-2

General weighting of criteria

The weights of the major criteria categories should vary on the basis of the type of deal being evaluated. In efficiency deals, price is far more important than in transformation deals, for instance.

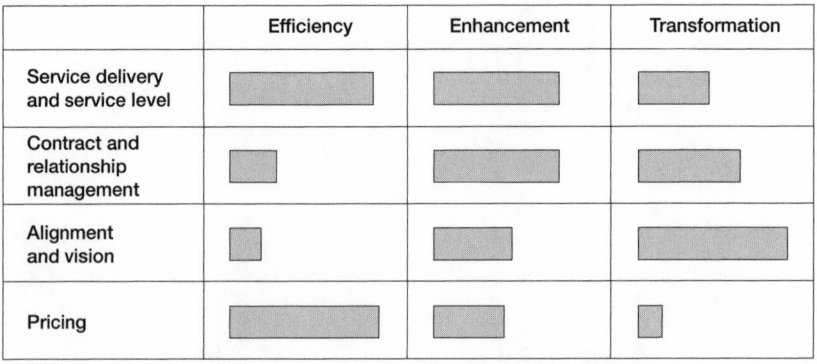

	Efficiency	Enhancement	Transformation
Service delivery and service level			
Contract and relationship management			
Alignment and vision			
Pricing			

Clearly, in an efficiency deal, pricing and service levels are far more important than in a transformation deal, where alignment and vision are far more important. Transformation deals typically have to be far more flexible, and the provider far more able to adapt to your organization and change in the relationship. The weightings for each criterion need to be determined by consensus among your team. Make sure that in your planning, you allow at least a day to create the criteria and organization of your hierarchy and another day to come to consensus on weights for the criteria.

Finally, you'll need to agree on a scoring system. This may seem like an obvious task, but we find many selection processes thrown off because the evaluation team has not at the outset agreed on how proposals will be scored. You can use any scoring mechanism that suits your organization and your team; just make sure you discuss what it is. This discussion needs to focus particularly on two issues: what the scores mean and who is allowed to score certain criteria. To normalize scoring across the diverse group that will be participating in the evaluation, discuss the range of scores that you will use. To make sure the participants understand the scoring system, you should create some scenarios to show where each score would be applied. Also determine whether you want everyone on the team scoring every criterion—you may very well want to limit scoring on service delivery and service levels to your experts on that topic while not having these experts score issues related to relationship and contract management.

Receive and Score Written Responses, and Conduct Oral Interviews

The next activity in the Fast Track process is to score the providers' written responses to the provider packet once these responses arrive. Beyond following the scoring mechanisms that you have just created, you'll now create a list of questions and clarifications of the providers' responses. This list will serve as your guideline during the oral presentation.

The oral presentation is the first chance for your evaluation team to begin to assess cultural fit with the various providers. Since this is such

an important factor in so many service relationships, we strongly recommend that the oral presentations be led by the provider's relationship manager who would manage the ongoing relationship. Similarly,
the discussions of service delivery should be led by the provider's service delivery personnel. You might note that this leaves little role for the
service providers' salespeople and contract-negotiation team, and you're
right. These individuals will not have to live with the relationship, and
so they should not have a significant role in the presentations.

The second stage of the oral response process should include innovation workshops. We stress the inclusion of these workshops as part of
the evaluation for each type of deal, because change is inevitable. During the course of your relationship with the service provider that you
select, your needs, the industry, your business strategies, your markets,
your customers, the economic climate, and technology will all change.
Consequently, your relationship and your service delivery must change
as well, if you are to achieve the agility and growth goals of Multisourcing. Innovation workshops allow you to examine in a structured way the
service providers' capabilities to drive change. Certainly, innovation will
generally be more important in transformation deals than in efficiency
deals, but even efficiency deals should deliver value through innovation.

To run an innovation workshop, you'll need to create two or three
likely change scenarios—envision what sort of changes your organization might undergo over the next two to five years. Examples include a
change in executive leadership, entering new markets or locations,
acquiring another organization or being acquired, and a significant
increase or decrease in the workforce. As you work on your scenarios,
try to make sure the change affects the majority of the service levels you
have created and several of the comanagement processes.

Each change scenario for the innovation workshop should be
described in no more than a single page and should include a description of how you envision that the change will affect your service needs.
Provide these to the service providers, and ask them to present their
approach to handling this change within the context of your relationship. Make sure that you specify that you are not asking them to provide a price for a changed level of service, but to show how they would

handle the change—which may or may not include a renegotiation of price. Make sure that you deliver the change scenarios in such a way that each service provider has the same amount of time before it presents its response. Again, require that the response be delivered by the relationship manager and service personnel who will be involved with your organization, not by a salesperson. It will also be important to document what the provider promises, or even says, during these presentations—you will most likely want to update your SoWs to reflect these statements.

You'll score each provider on the basis of your impression of its capability to respond to change appropriately. Add these scores to your evaluation model. As we've previously mentioned, while innovation is more critical to enhancement and transformation than efficiency deals, efficiency deals are not immune to change, so innovation workshops and scoring remain an important part of those selection processes. To recognize the increased importance of innovation, and of relationships, in enhancement and transformation deals, we also recommend having an additional change scenario that is delivered to the provider during its presentation and that requires it to react in real time. This will give you insight into how the provider's team works under pressure and how the various members of the team work together—a vital consideration for these types of deals.

Due Diligence

The final piece of your evaluation will be the due diligence checks, which verify that the providers' answers are accurate and complete. One of the major factors to evaluate during due diligence is each provider's financial position. The other major factors are reference checks and site visits. We strongly recommend taking the time to interview the providers' references. Insist up front that reference accounts have as much similarity to your situation as possible (services delivered, level of customization, sourcing model, industry, company size, etc.). Many clients we speak to skip this step, assuming that the references are all positive and won't have anything interesting to say. This has never been our experience, however. Every reference-check conversation yields interesting information when you focus your discussions on relationship management, change management, and innovation. Given that these capabilities are the bedrocks of Multisourcing success, it is critical to have these conversations. Specifically, we recommend that that you make multiple levels of contact with the participants' references (CEO to CEO, service executive to service executive, delivery manager to delivery manager) and that you always ask what the reference would change about its deal. We also recommend doing some homework and finding one or more of each provider's clients that are not on the reference list and taking the time to learn about those relationships as well.

You should also plan for time to visit the providers' service delivery sites (if all work is performed on-site, visit a customer with a similar arrangement). John Howard (a pseudonym), a sourcing executive managing a large IT outsourcing contract at a government agency, performed an evaluation that included site visits. "But we didn't visit a current customer who had the same help desk needs we did. The provider had a quite impressive operation but, we later discovered, didn't have any customers with similar requirements to ours. We thought we'd done our due diligence in the site visit, but we missed that important factor. It took the provider much longer to ramp up to our needs than we had anticipated based on the site visit we did perform."

You should also allow time for the providers to perform their own due diligence and verify that what you have presented as your service needs, baselines, assets, and personnel is complete. Some organizations try to avoid this level of disclosure, but it is simply another part of building a successful relationship. Any surprises that the provider encounters will delay or derail the delivery of the expected business outcomes—and that hurts you as much as, if not more than, it hurts the provider. The best service providers will insist on detailed due diligence. You should consider this insistence a positive reflection of their commitment to meeting your needs.

With the scores you assign from due diligence, oral presentations, responses to questions, and the innovation workshops, you should be ready to complete your scoring and select the provider or providers that you will enter final negotiations with. That's the fourth and final activity of the Fast Track process.

Evaluating an Offshore Provider

THE EVALUATION of offshore providers should not differ materially from the evaluation of domestic providers. If you've followed the sourcing strategy process, you will have evaluated and accepted the different risks that come with choosing nondomestic provision of services. Several items, however, deserve special attention and will be discussed here, before we move on to the negotiation phase of Fast Track. Because nondomestic sourcing involves extensive change to the standard in-person processes and services delivery at most organizations, and because the providers are usually less familiar, you need to apply more due diligence to your selection. The ability to adapt to new providers, new resource pools, new processes, and new methods of service delivery, as well as a willingness to embrace partnerships with external service providers—often from a totally different culture—is vital. In our experience, we have seen clients pay either too much or not enough attention to the following factors when they are considering an offshore provider:

- *Certifications:* Keep in mind that process- and quality-certification standards are largely driven not by the consumers of services and products but by the producers—thus certifications are designed to meet providers' needs rather than those of users. For this reason, do not put your trust in certifications, but in proven examples of competence. One common certification heralded by offshore providers is the capability maturity model (CMM, which has levels of 1 through 5). CMM measures an organization's capability to manage its software development— how well it can quantitatively measure its efforts, and its understanding of the meaning of various metrics. The model does not measure actual competence in software development.

Thus, it is theoretically possible that a provider with a CMM level 5 certification simply has rock-solid management processes in place that show that the organization is not very good at application development. So, be aware of and require the relevant certifications (such as CMM, ITIL, and Six Sigma), but also be aware of what the certifications really mean.

- *On-site presentations:* Your evaluation should always include on-site presentations by the providers (as described in this chapter), and this step should not change when you are evaluating offshore providers. It is even more critical, however, that the ongoing relationship manager and delivery managers be present and participate in these presentations.

- *Site visits:* Another absolute requirement, particularly if this is your first experience with offshore sourcing in this particular location, is a visit to the site where the service delivery work will be performed. Your evaluation team needs this visit to adequately understand both the nature of the relationship that will develop and to gain a visceral understanding of any geography-specific risks. When you visit the country, you will also want to pay attention to and experience its cultural attributes. At the service provider's facilities, you will want to see and inspect the work environments and meet the employees.

- *Distance:* One major issue that enterprises will face when selecting offshore providers is the impact of large differences in time zones and significant physical distance. In the selection process, make sure you understand where decision-making authority resides within the offshore firm, as this will affect the responsiveness of the provider. If the individuals with authority are located offshore, you may experience delays in major decisions. These delays will not be satisfactory if you need rapid decisions.

- *Price:* Nondomestic delivery has typically focused on low labor costs—but labor cost is only a part of the overall cost of a service. Not all work can be done offshore, and offshore delivery incurs additional costs. When working with your business case, be sure to include possible additional costs for network bandwidth for the transfer of information to and from the offshore location, as well as travel costs for your services and relationship managers to make regular site visits. These costs will not necessarily be a large factor in your overall costs, but need to be factored into your return on investment and business-case expectations so that you have accurate data to measure success. IndyMac Bank calculates and tracks both a gross and a net savings from nondomestic services. The gross savings look solely at labor cost differences, which the bank calculates to be slightly more than 50 percent versus domestic labor. Then management, technology, and systems costs related to offshore provision are subtracted (which account for around 10 percent of costs), yielding a net savings of 40 percent.

- *Security:* You should evaluate the security of offshore providers just as you do for onshore providers, while exploring additional security risks. We find that many clients spend far too much time worried about IT security while ignoring the other, perhaps more important, security-related issues of offshore service provision. Most well-known offshore providers have invested considerably in their IT security. It is therefore more important to evaluate issues such as personnel hiring and background checks, the physical security of delivery sites, local law enforcement issues, and local regulatory processes that may allow foreign governments access to confidential data.

- *Financials:* Part of due diligence is always assessing the financial health of the providers. Doing so for nondomestic providers often requires specialty expertise, as different countries have different accounting standards and disclosure regulations. This is another area for which you may want to consider engaging external experts who are thoroughly familiar with the financial landscape in the country of the providers you are evaluating.

- *Jurisdiction:* Your contracts should specify that contract disputes fall under the jurisdiction of your local offices, not the service delivery location. You also need to ensure that the service provider has assets in the local jurisdiction where disputes will be resolved so that in the worst-case scenario, legal action will carry actual repercussions for the service provider.

- *Staffing retention and attrition issues:* Increasingly, many non-domestic providers are experiencing higher attrition rates in their local countries, which may affect performance on individual projects. Discuss employee issues with your prospective provider, and ask how it addresses attrition issues and what steps it is taking to ensure continuity of skills and staffing.

- *Culture:* Cultural intelligence involves more than simply recognizing that cultural differences exist. Working across cultures is not easy; there will inevitably be cultural misunderstandings and miscommunications. Some of the cultural differences may be addressed in the selection process. Over the longer term, however, a robust cross-cultural program will help your organization mitigate the risk of working with cultural and language differences. You should evaluate the offshore provider's willingness and capability to help bridge the culture divide.

- *Vision:* Finally, you will want to understand the long-term vision and strategies of your prospective offshore providers in terms of technology, vertical competency, and business-solutions approaches. This discussion should also include plans for expanded geographic presence and risk management via dispersal of resources

Fast Track Phase Four: Negotiate

IN THIS SECTION, we do not intend to provide a guide to negotiation. There are already many excellent books and courses devoted to negotiation. Here, we briefly want to touch on some of the unique factors of negotiating a services contract within a Fast Track context. We'll focus on two elements: who is involved in negotiation from both the recipient and the provider sides, and some basic services-negotiation strategy.

Who Is in the Room

One key element of negotiation for services is making sure that the right parties are in the room. Sharon Huang (a pseudonym), a general manager at a nonprofit institute, learned this lesson the hard way. "During negotiations, we focused on the transition process since we were moving from one external partner to another. Our new provider's negotiation team seemed to be terrific to deal with," Huang notes. "They committed to a number of specific time frames and deliverables during the transition process. Unfortunately, the people making the commitments weren't the people who would end up managing the transition—who, once they got on site, told us the commitments that had been made were impossible to meet. By that time, of course, we'd negotiated the exit plan with our old provider based on those deliverables. Our transition was a mess, and our new service relationship couldn't have gotten off to a worse start."

So, who should be on the negotiation teams? From the service provider side, two groups must be present: (1) the relationship management and service delivery teams, and (2) the decision makers. Now these two groups may be one and the same, but not necessarily so. The first group must be present to ensure that they know and approve of the commitments being made. Huang's experience is not an isolated incident. We see innumerable cases of sales and contract teams making commitments that service delivery teams would never have acceded to. While you need to have the service delivery and relationship management team present to provide a check on the commitments being made, these groups may or may not be empowered to make decisions during negotiation. Never negotiate a services contract without having in the room the individuals who can approve agreements on the spot.

Your negotiation team needs to include enough members to cover a variety of needed competencies. Of course, you'll need representatives to cover each of six comanagement processes as well as experts in the service area and representatives of the key recipient constituencies. Ensure that a representative of the financial team that helped build the business case in your sourcing action plan is there to evaluate the effect of pricing proposals and financial engineering on the business case. You will also probably want a procurement specialist on your negotiation team.

Additionally, some specific individuals should be part of your negotiation team. These include your relationship manager, who will be the primary point of contact with the service provider; a representative from the sourcing office or sourcing council to ensure compliance with sourcing maxims and enterprise sourcing strategy; and the most senior applicable business unit or service-recipient executive. Ensuring the executive involvement of service consumers will go a long way to guaranteeing customer satisfaction with the service in the future—a key measurement of success once the deal is implemented. This level of participation helps the service-consumer community understand the particular trade-offs that will inevitably have to be made in the negotiation.

Negotiation Strategy

Before you enter negotiations, your team needs to create a negotiation strategy. Your goal is to always be in control of the negotiation process, ensuring that the provider is responding to you and not the other way around. Doing so requires keeping the provider's perspective and motivations in the front of your team's mind at all times. In general, an external service provider's goals in forming a new relationship are relatively straightforward—create a predictable revenue stream, at the maximum profit, with the minimum risk. (Sometimes, of course, the provider will purposely agree to pricing that does not provide profit; see "External Service Providers and Profit.") Every part of the provider's negotiation will be driven toward achieving these goals. Your goals are not contradictory to these. You want predictable costs, at a reasonable profit for the provider, with minimum risk for you. Balancing the risks between provider and recipient and determining what is reasonable profit based on who assumes what risks is the heart of the negotiation process.

EXTERNAL SERVICE PROVIDERS AND PROFIT

We return to the dangerous myth of the enemy. Because you are entering a service relationship, the profitability of your service provider is of significant concern. Unlike a one-time acquisition of tangible goods, a situation in which the long-term viability of the vendor is largely irrelevant, a services sourcing relationship usually means that you will rely on the external service provider for months and years after the contract is signed. Thus, you want to ensure first and foremost that your service provider is sound financially and compliant fiscally and, second, that the provider is making a profit on your deal so that it stays in business and can afford to invest in innovation and improvement. Service providers have a close watch on profitability at the deal level. The last thing you want in a service relationship is a provider that needs to cut corners because of thin margins on your deal; if the provider needs to save money, your quality of services and personnel will invariably suffer. Even in an efficiency relationship, getting a rock-bottom price is rarely a long-term positive.

Be aware, though, that you may encounter providers that propose unprofitable pricing. This most often occurs when a service provider is trying to buy its way into a particular industry or class of services. Being a provider's guinea pig can be very appealing when you are looking only at the dollar figures, but may not mean good things for service delivery and business outcomes. On the other hand, being the first reference account can give you much more pull and can guarantee you get high-quality services at low cost. Be aware of this pricing dynamic, and make sure you understand the service provider's motivations and the risks of entering a deal in such circumstances.

If you've chosen a prime-contractor or consortia model, you'll need to examine the profitability of all the providers involved in delivering your services. It's just as dangerous to have your prime contractor treating other service providers as the enemy as it is for you to do so.

Your negotiation team also needs to create a schedule for negotiations and a target completion date. Don't become a hostage to this target date, however. We have been involved in countless contract renegotiations that have been needed because the service recipient made the wrong compromises to meet the target dates. Keep in mind the mantra "No deal is better than a bad deal."

One important aspect of the negotiation schedule is the order of the issues. Do not let the service provider take the lead here. Decide before you get to the table what your priority issues are and how you would like to address them. In fact, it's a good idea to formally document the desired and minimally acceptable positions on each of these issues before beginning your negotiations.

You'll also want to make sure that everyone on the team knows who has decision-making authority over what parts of the contract. This authority may go to a single member of the team or different members for different aspects of the contract, but everyone on your team should know exactly who has final authority for whatever issue is being discussed.

A few final notes on preparing your negotiation strategy:

- Determine in advance who will play the standard negotiation roles of good cop and bad cop.

- Always keep in mind that outsourcing is not just a business decision; it is an emotional issue. Expect emotions to come up during the negotiation process, and plan for them.

- Remember to treat your negotiation team humanely—give them breaks and time to debrief and discuss issues privately. The results will be much better.

- Regarding current service delivery, always expect that negotiations will fail—and that your current service delivery will have to remain in place. One of the most common mistakes we see is clients assuming that once they are in the final negotiations, a deal is inevitable. They therefore begin to make the transition before the deal is done; this simply hands more negotiating power to the provider.

- Finally, do not allow any to-be-decided points or any postcontract discovery to be included in your contract. This is a tactic that many service providers use to limit their risk and shift additional risk onto the service recipient.

A Contract You (and They) Can Live With

THE ENTIRE GOAL of this process is to create a contract that you and the service provider can live with. If from the beginning, you do the hard work of defining a sourcing strategy, creating a service action plan, and closely defining your needs, then you will be well on your way to Multisourcing. Relationships and governance are far more important than any other factors in determining the future success of your sourcing decisions.

Making sure you stay on course, however, requires more than just a good contract and a solid relationship. It requires ongoing management and measurement of the right metrics, not just the easily available metrics. The next step toward living profitably with your contract is updating the business case in your service action plan—this will be one of the touchstone documents in measuring your success. In the next chapter, we'll look at the rest of the process of measuring success and creating a sourcing management dashboard to ensure you are still headed in the right direction and are making progress.

CHAPTER seven

Measure Your Progress

T HE TERM CAPTAIN'S LOG IS MOST KNOWN TODAY
from the famous beginning segments of the classic TV
show *Star Trek*. The term, however, originated with the first seafaring
voyages beyond view of land. While you can determine how far north or
south you've progressed using only the stars, you can only measure how
far east or west you have traveled with the help of precision timekeeping instruments. In the early days of nautical exploration (and up to the
1700s, when reliable maritime clocks were invented), the captain of a
ship traveling across an ocean literally carried a log on board. Several
times a day, the captain tied a rope to the log, threw it overboard from
the bow of the ship, and counted how long it took to reach the stern.
From this timing, the captain calculated a rough speed and then estimated how far the ship had traveled that day. The book he recorded
these measurements in took on the name of the instrument used—the
captain's log.[1]

As you can imagine, these measurements were horribly imprecise.
In a journey across oceans, the estimate was often wrong by a thousand
miles, and countless ships and lives were lost when a reef or another
obstruction suddenly appeared days before the captain expected it.

Outsourcing measurement in many cases is no more precise in measuring progress toward business goals than the captain's log. Measures, if they even exist, are imprecise and bear little relevance to business outcomes.

How can you measure your progress toward your required business outcomes? The goal is to create a Multisourcing analog of the modern global positioning system (more commonly known as GPS) that can help you with this measurement task. This is the third responsibility of the Multisourcing management office: the creation of standard measurements that illustrate the business value of sourcing actions. These metrics can then be brought together in a *Multisourcing dashboard,* an integrated measurement technique used to collect, track, and communicate the results of services, and to link these results to business outcomes, thereby illustrating business value. Using the dashboard allows all levels of enterprise management to gauge success according to their own criteria.

The process of measurement (including the continuous improvement that flows out of measurement) is the last piece of Multisourcing, but it is also the beginning. Measurement is an ongoing, cyclical set of activities. The measurement of current services feeds the sourcing strategy with the data needed to make decisions. For managing current providers, then, measurement is your first step, rather than your last.

This would seem to be the simplest and most straightforward part of managing Multisourcing—after all, what is management but measuring progress and adjusting inputs to create desired outputs? Unfortunately, though, we rarely find a client that has mastered the art of measuring its sourcing environment. Measurement processes, when they are even implemented at all, often break down under the following circumstances:

- Many measurement schemes start and end with pricing benchmarks and do not measure quality of service or service level achievement.

- When service levels are measured, many clients measure too much and get lost in the data.

- Service level measurements are often built around what is easy to measure rather than true indicators of service value and performance.

- The measurements do not take into account innovation and continuous improvement.

- The measurements ignore metrics relevant to service consumers.

- The measurements overlook the relationship factors that are a far better indicator of business outcomes.

In this chapter, we'll look in detail at how to set up an effective Multisourcing measurement practice. We'll cover how to determine what to measure and how to create an integrated Multisourcing dashboard that delivers the needed information to all levels of the enterprise and feeds the sourcing strategy process.

The Big Picture: The Governance of Evaluation and the Design of Measurement

THE GOVERNANCE of sourcing evaluation, as we discussed in chapter 4, encompasses delineating the authority for measurement—how are service providers measured, and how is success and failure determined? One of our key themes, that Multisourcing is built on relationships, means that your governance of measurement needs to specify how to not only measure quantitative performance, but also value measures. In short, evaluation governance must define standards for measuring relationships and develop the approaches and competencies to use measurement to create continuous improvement. The first aspect, though, is the evaluation and measurement process itself.

As noted, one of the chief failings in many attempts to measure outsourced environments is that they do not take continuous improvement into account; they simply crunch numbers, calculate an incentive or a fee reduction, and move on. Effective sourcing evaluation governance requires defining a four-phase approach that links with several of the comanagement processes. The four phases are *define and measure, examine, correct,* and *guide.*

Define and Measure

The first phase is the literal process of measurement. In the statements of work you created while selecting, and negotiating with, providers, you should have defined your required service levels and your behavioral expectations of the service providers. Ideally, your contract also includes benchmarking clauses. Now you need to get down to the nitty-gritty—who measures, who benchmarks, who audits, and how often are each of these processes performed? The measurement phase feeds the information required to the equity and the audit and assessment comanagement processes. Measurement takes the guesswork out of management and allows a focus on quantitative measures of performance. This phase is just the beginning, but it is where most governance systems stop.

Examine

The second phase, *examine,* is not so much about identifying success and failures for the purpose of calculating fee reductions and incentives (although that is part of it), but about identifying the root causes of missed service levels, inadequate relationship processes, or other failures. Who will perform these analyses? How will the results be presented, and to whom? Most often, the provider leads this examination, with users participating in the process. The examine phase supports the audit and assessment, equity, and communication and feedback comanagement processes.

Correct

In this phase, the results of the measure and examine phases are used as the basis for correcting flawed activities and processes. Correction is accomplished by generating, selecting, designing, testing, and implementing improvements. Your process design should include representation from service consumers and service providers as well as any appropriate staff from the Multisourcing management office. The service provider generally documents and implements the corrective action and reports the correction to all participating parties. The correction phase supports the responsibility and integration comanagement processes and provides vital input to future investment decisions.

Guide

Following the implementation of corrective actions, the service provider and recipient must work together to continuously guide the activity or process. This helps the parties ensure compliance and maintain the gains achieved through the correction process. The guide phase should include the creation of rules for monitoring service delivery changes, the documentation of results and lessons learned, and the application of lessons to other aspects of service delivery. This phase supports the audit and assessment, communication and feedback, and integration comanagement processes.

Traditional Measurement: Service Levels, Price, and Value

ONCE THE FOUR PHASES of measurement are designed, the next step is to define and begin collecting data on the actual measures for each of the services being measured. Traditionally, these measures have focused on price and service levels (which have most often been completely focused on technical or operational metrics). Because these remain critical components of Multisourcing performance measurement, it is worth spending some time discussing how these measures should be handled.

If you did not define service levels as part of the evaluation and negotiation process discussed in chapter 6, this is, of course, the first place to start. In conjunction with service providers, you will have to define these service levels for any existing relationships that do not have them as yet (see chapter 6 for some direction in establishing service levels).

Keep in mind as you begin the measurement process that establishing fewer measures that are consistently focused on business impact will yield better results. Using too many service levels is an all-too-common mistake. Measuring fewer service levels helps you and the service provider focus on key outcomes and therefore improves results. As you review the contracted service levels you have already created or are planning to put in place, keep these rules in mind:

1. Having fewer, more meaningful measures gives greater focus and, therefore, greater deal success.

2. To be an effective tool to drive service provider behavior, SLAs must have fee reductions (often called penalties) associated with underperformance.

3. Fee reductions must be significant (10 percent to 20 percent of contracted price) to effect behavioral change.

4. Focusing fee reductions over fewer measures helps guide the service provider into appropriate behaviors.

Of course, from a business perspective, measuring service levels without reference to the cost of achieving those levels is irrelevant. Start by comparing the cost per service level to your baselines measured during your sourcing strategy process. This is the first step toward gaining insight into business value and the achievement of required outcomes. Have the assumptions and projections of the sourcing business case been achieved? Have costs been reduced? Has value been delivered?

These quantitative comparisons are impossible if you are evaluating an existing service relationship that had neither baselines nor a business case prepared. In these situations, the first priority is to begin measurement immediately. From there, you can start to measure trends and set goals for improvement from these "new" baselines.

This question of value also needs to be put into perspective via external benchmarks. This is why we recommend including a benchmarking clause in your contracts. While it is important to understand the performance of a service provider in relation to baselines, understanding the business value of your sourcing relationships also depends on understanding the market rates for your required service levels. The equity comanagement process depends on this market benchmarking to make determinations of fair compensation and fair value for all the parties involved in the relationship.

Measure Your Relationship

AFTER MEASURING the basics of service level and price, it's time to turn to the second generation of service measures—measures that are just as important for ensuring that you stay on course in your Multisourcing journey: the quality of your relationships with service providers. We call these measures a relationship performance assessment. While relationship measures are qualitative as opposed to the quantitative measures of service levels and price, they are no less important.

The place to turn to find the most appropriate relationship measures is back to your selection and evaluation process. There, you created a set of prioritized evaluation criteria. Remarkably, many organizations don't consider using these criteria as the basis for their ongoing measurement of service providers. Earlier in the book, we advised that your criterion hierarchy include four major categories: price, service delivery and service level, contract and relationship, and alignment and vision. The traditional measures discussed in the preceding section cover price and service level. Don't forget that once you are in the relationship, you should not spend time or effort measuring the *how* of delivery, but should only consider the outcomes as expressed in SLAs. To round out your measurement picture, you need to create ongoing metrics to cover the remaining two criteria: contract and relationship, and alignment and vision.

We need to mention customer service as a key metric. In general, customer service should be a part of your SLAs and therefore will be measured as part of service level. However, if you do not include customer service in your SLAs, you need to add it to your relationship metrics. The satisfaction level of service consumers needs to be a key driver of service provider behavior—this can only occur if it is included in your measures.

For the two criteria not yet addressed (contract and relationship, and alignment and vision), the metrics that you use will depend on how exactly you broke out your criteria model. Following our example from chapter 6 (see figure 6-1), you would use a metric related to your governance SoW to measure the relationship criterion. If you've implemented the six comanagement processes, then the metrics here are straightforward. You can rank, using a simple scoring system (perhaps the same one that you used in the evaluation), the provider's engagement in, and value added to, each of the comanagement processes. We provide some interactive tools to help with this process at www.gartnerpress.com/multisourcing. Given that these are qualitative measures, you may want to consider engaging a third party to perform the evaluation to guarantee objectivity.

In the alignment and vision category, using our example criterion hierarchy, you would create measures for the alignment with business objectives and quality or amount of innovation, at the very least. To measure the alignment of business objectives, you will want to examine the service provider's progress in meeting its own enterprise goals and assess whether its progress accords with your expectations and changing needs. During the evaluation, you should also have set some goals and expectations for innovation—what kind of innovation you expect the service provider to deliver (improved service, greater efficiency, lower cost, higher productivity). Be sure to measure the service provider against the achievement of the explicit expectations from your selection process. Again, as these may be qualitative assessments, you should consider engaging a mutually agreeable outside party to assist in these evaluations.

Creating a complete set of second-generation measures is a lengthy process that requires many iterations. DuPont has spent seven years creating a balanced scorecard that is common across all its IT service providers. This does not mean that the actual metrics are the same for both the data network and application support, but means that the categories of measures are common. Specifically, DuPont uses five high-level categories: financial performance, contract performance, service delivery, process execution, and improvement initiative (recognizing the need for continuous improvement). Then each category is broken down appropriately for the service category. There are common measures for each service as well, such as service availability, service reliability, and responsiveness, all of which fall under service delivery.

The final aspect of measuring relationships deserves special attention because it is the bedrock of Multisourcing relationships—trust.

Trust and Control: Measuring Confidence in Your Relationships

ONE OF THE KEY THEMES in this book has been the nature of sourcing relationships and the trust that is an absolute requirement for these relationships to thrive. Trust is a vital element of any relationship; without trust, in fact, there is no relationship, just two adversaries. A study we conducted in 2001 revealed the importance of trust in sourcing decisions. When asked about the importance of trust in their decision making, 93 percent of service managers said that trust was "highly important," the highest category possible.

The difficult thing about trust, though, is that it is typically built or undermined through informal, even subconscious, interactions between the parties in a relationship. Our study revealed that service managers began forming their impression of the trustworthiness of service provider organizations on the basis of their first contact with a salesperson. We repeat: *service managers said that a single conversation with a single employee created an impression of the trustworthiness of the entire service provider organization.*

We believe that trust is far too important to the success of service relationships to be left to informal, subconscious, or intuitive measures.

While we may not be able to exactly quantify trust, we can add some rigor to the qualitative measurements.

There is a flip side of trust as well: control. Or as Ronald Reagan put it, "Trust, but verify." Sourcing relationships are not personal relationships; they are business relationships. Consequently, trust must be balanced by appropriate controls and verification. If you've created appropriate governance for the coordination of service, implemented the six comanagement processes, and have developed ways to assess service levels and pricing, you have formalized many of the control mechanisms. But control is not enough for relationships; trust must also exist. Successful relationships are defined by the right mix of trust and control. However, that still leaves the question of assessing the state of trust in your relationships.

To follow up on our 2001 study, we have embarked on ongoing research to establish ways of measuring trust in sourcing relationships on a continuous basis. This research has identified ten key components of trust essential to the relationship between a service provider and a service recipient and the ten most common relationship control mechanisms (tables 7-1 and 7-2).[2] We used the control mechanisms as a least common denominator for our survey; the use of the six comanagement processes is not yet common, whereas control mechanisms were more broadly understood.

A Confidence Index

You can ascertain the level of confidence in a relationship by having various parties score their agreement or disagreement with each of the ten components of both trust and control. We use a scale that ranges from −5 (strongly disagree) to +5 (strongly agree). Each component is phrased as a question; the respondents assign a score based on their agreement. Some typical questions include the following:

- Does your service provider have the capability to deliver? Is the service provider dependable?

- Is the service provider compatible with the enterprise? Is the service provider's reputation strong?

TABLE 7-1

The components of trust in sourcing relationships

Our 2001 study determined the ten components of trust. These components form the foundation of a strong relationship between a service provider and recipient.

Trust component	Definition
Capability	The technical, management, and financial skills and resources to do the job
Congruency	The match between perception and reality
Predictability	The ability to set and meet expectations such as financial certainty, financial stability, and delivering to targets
Dependability	The ability of parties to anticipate how the other will perform and behave, particularly in changing and unpredictable circumstances
Mutuality	A shared commitment to a common goal
Communications	Giving and receiving the correct information in a meaningful and timely way
Consistency	The ability to understand standards, processes, and protocols and to apply them consistently
Responsiveness	The ability and willingness to understand and respond to new circumstances and to harness skills and resources to meet new needs
Compatibility	The match between the recipient's business needs and culture and the provider's delivery models and culture
Reputation	An established track record of success verified by many sources

- Does your enterprise have adequate decision making?

- Does your enterprise effectively use benchmarking?

By tabulating the average of scores, you gain a measure of the current state of confidence in the relationship.

Working with many clients to score the level of confidence in their service relationships, we have found that relationship confidence falls into six levels:

Organizational trust: Scores are 3 or higher. Trust extends beyond individual relationships or groups to the entire organization. Significant personnel change will not have an immediate effect on trust.

Group trust: Scores range from 1.5 to 3. Trust extends throughout the groups that interact with the service provider. Some personnel change can be managed without damaging trust.

TABLE 7-2

Typical control mechanisms in sourcing relationships

The ten most common control mechanisms in sourcing were identified in our 2001 study. The balance of trust and control creates or undermines confidence in sourcing relationships. We've related the control mechanisms to the comanagement processes from chapter 4.

Control	Comanagement process	Examples
Feedback	Communication and feedback	• Predict changes, risks, or other issues that could affect a service or project. • Monitor key performance indicators.
Decision making	Strategy	• Institute simple and reliable approvals process. • Set clear delegation limits.
Setting goals and standards	Integration	• Set key performance indicators and working practices. • Impose, or accept, technical standards.
Setting roles and responsibilities	Responsibility	• Define an integrated set of activities that constitute end-to-end service, who will do each activity, and who will be accountable.
Managing change	Strategy	• Predict, plan, evaluate, and prioritize potential changes, and assess associated benefits and risks.
Managing behavior	Audit and assessment	• Make use of service credits, gain-sharing incentives, and sanctions.
Financial management	Equity	• Identify all costs and manage to budget. • Set and control contingencies.
Ensuring continuous improvement	Audit and assessment	• Implement and measure selected improvements. • Continuously identify opportunities for improvement in costs, service levels, and management.
Ensuring peer-group parity	Equity	• Benchmark price and service levels.
Managing demand	Strategy	• Balance requirements with costs. • Prioritize.

Individual trust: Scores range from 0 to 1.5. Trust exists at a basic level but generally only between those specific individuals who work together; if these individuals change, the trust relationship can deteriorate quickly.

Individual distrust: Scores range from 0 to −1.5. Trust is failing between the individuals involved; there is more reliance on formal controls and penalties than on proactive problem resolution. Changes in personnel may help revive the relationship.

Group distrust: Scores range from −1.5 to −3. Trust has failed between the groups most involved in managing the relationship. Reviving the relationship will require significant intervention by executive management.

Organizational distrust: Scores are −3 and below. Trust has totally failed. The relationship cannot be revived. Exit planning has begun.

As you may suspect, the level of trust may vary significantly between the operational level—those involved in service delivery—and the executive level (the CEO, board of directors, and business unit heads). This is often the case when a service provider has entered the organization not through the process of strategy, governance, and evaluation but through executive mandate. Executive-level trust, however, can change exceedingly quickly when the realities of performance are presented. In one relationship we assessed, board-level trust moved from group trust to organizational distrust within a two-hour meeting in which pricing and service level benchmarks were presented. On the basis of data presented, the members of the board perceived that they had been misled by executives of the service provider. The service managers had already lost trust in the service provider because of poor service delivery, but could not get the board's attention to explain problems until these external benchmarks were presented.

Of course, operational-level trust is also susceptible to change over time on the basis of performance and the achievement of desired outcomes. When the comanagement processes are working well, confidence increases; when confidence increases, comanagement performs better. Thus, operational trust can create a virtuous cycle that keeps a relationship performing at a high level.

Several confidence disrupters, however, can quickly change the momentum of trust. The disruption can then begin a downward spiral in which the falling confidence limits the effectiveness of comanagement. These limitations of comanagement then impede the achievement of goals, which in turn erodes trust. Three common situations often disrupt confidence:

1. *Financial engineering that is not well understood:* In the latter stages of a long-term deal in which significant financial engineering has changed cost structures, the costs of service relative to market pricing can increase dramatically. At this stage, the implicit loans that the service provider has made to lower upfront costs have to be repaid. When this change from relative low cost to relative high cost occurs without the understanding of key managers and executives, doubts about service value appear. These doubts then rapidly undermine trust.

2. *Transition from enhancement or transformation deals to efficiency deals:* Throughout the book, we have noted that at some point in the life of every enhancement or transformation deal, expectations will change. The service recipient will begin to expect that performance improvements will be consolidated and that costs will begin to be controlled—in essence, the recipient expects the deal to become an efficiency deal. If this change is not planned for, or if the inflection point is not mutually agreed upon and communicated, the perceived performance of a relationship will change rapidly and undermine trust.

3. *Inability by either party to shift from customization to standardization:* Many outsourcing relationships are built around the expected cost savings that come with moving to a standardized environment. Often in practice, however, the service recipient is unprepared for standardization (even though the recipient committed to standardization in theory) or the provider has inadequate experience in managing the transition. In either

case, outcomes can swing rapidly and drag trust down so quickly that comanagement processes struggle to recover.

In general, the factors that disrupt confidence fall into six categories: lack of compatibility between service provider and service recipient; lack of leadership from service recipient executives who disengage once the deal is signed; lack of communication, particularly the communication of change in the service recipient's business needs; lack of skilled resources to manage the relationship; misaligned expectations between needs and actually contracted services; and misalignment between deal type and actual need. You will note how closely these disrupters correspond to the myths that lead to outsourcing problems that we presented in the introduction.

Using Trust to Assess and Manage Relationships

Clearly, you can use the trust levels as part of your assessment of the quality of each of your relationships. Trust is an integral part of managing the many outsourcing relationships that go along with Multisourcing—particularly when integrated with the six comanagement processes. The trust ratings, though, are also very helpful in assessing the current state of outsourcing relationships that preceded your current sourcing strategy or your implementation of comanagement processes. Trying to establish comanagement with a service provider in which you or your organization has little trust may be counterproductive. So, in assessing your existing relationships, the best place to start is the combination of price and service benchmarks and the trust index.

Our research has found that it is possible to resuscitate relationships with very low operational-trust scores (around -2) if executive-level trust remains high (1 or above). These are the first service relationships to target for improvement—but time is of the essence. As soon as executive-level trust begins to fall, it will be too late to turn things around.

We have worked with many clients that have used the trust index as the basis for repairing a relationship in these circumstances. For example, AutoCo, an international manufacturer and distributor of automobile parts, after struggling with several key outsourcing relationships, used the trust index to create comanagement processes and to save two service relationships that are now meeting business needs effectively. When AutoCo evaluated trust for these service providers, the providers scored near and just below zero. The low scores were particularly the result of very low scores in the mutuality and congruency components depicted in table 7-1. Low scores in these components suggest a mismatch in deal types. As it turned out, several business units had different deal types in mind for the service providers. Where one business unit was expecting enhancement, another was expecting efficiency. The service providers were caught in the middle. The trust scores were used to bring together the service providers and the business units in an ad hoc strategy comanagement process. This meeting not only created consensus on goals, but also created executive support for building the rest of the comanagement processes. Outcomes and trust rapidly improved.

When operational trust is higher than executive trust, the proper value metrics are usually not being measured or appropriately communicated to executive management. The priority in these cases should be on developing and implementing audit and assessment and communication and feedback comanagement processes and the building of an appropriate executive-level sourcing dashboard (which we'll discuss shortly).

When both operational and board-level trust is low, save the time and effort of trying to resuscitate the relationship. Once trust in both areas has reached negative territory, it is virtually impossible to rebuild the relationship. No one will commit the necessary resources to fix something he or she believes is irreparably broken. You will be better served to use management time and effort on creating an exit plan, and beginning the process of selecting a new provider on the basis of your sourcing strategy and sourcing action plans.

By including evaluations of trust, you can gain a complete view of the state of all your relationships in your multisourced environment. Combining trust with benchmarks of price and service levels, assessments of alignment and vision, and innovation, you have a set of measures that matter and will guide your Multisourcing efforts.

Build a Dashboard

THE CONCEPT of a performance dashboard isn't new to most managers. However, Multisourcing dashboards are relatively uncommon. Organizations often measure the performance of various services, whether insourced or outsourced, at the technical level. They fail, however, to link these technical measures to business results, thereby rendering the measures meaningless to the senior managers of the enterprise and of no use in communicating the success of Multisourcing. A Multisourcing dashboard is a mechanism to collect, track, and communicate the results of various key services and to link these results to business outcomes, thereby illustrating the relative value of a service to business performance.[3] Dashboards are excellent tools for developing internal communications about the value of Multisourcing. The first step in building a dashboard is to create linked value measures

Linking Value Measures

Your Multisourcing dashboard starts with all the metrics that were just described and that cover the performance of each service relative to price, service levels, innovation, trust, and comanagement. Those sets of measures are necessary to drive the performance of each service and ensure that specific business goals are met. The Multisourcing dashboard is focused on overall Multisourcing performance, not just the performance of an individual service. Therefore, to create a dashboard, you need to link the value of all the services in your multisourced portfolio to business outcome values.

The hard work in creating these links has been done already if you've proceeded through the sourcing strategy process. During that process, you defined business strategies, business maxims, and sourcing maxims. As we discussed, maxims create a trail of evidence between sourcing actions and business strategy. Here is where you follow that trail. Your sourcing maxims guided your determination of outcomes when you created a sourcing action plan for the service. These outcomes in turn became service levels. By assembling each of these steps in reverse—service levels, outcomes, sourcing maxims, business maxims, business strategies—you can link even infrastructure service level measures to business-value measures.

You can also think of this process as a value chain. For example, IT infrastructure supports IT applications, which support business processes, which support business strategy, which supports business solutions or outcomes. By using such a value chain, you can create a set of linked measures. Figure 7-1 displays this linking process with examples of value measures for each level of the sample value chain. By combining all these linked metrics, you can provide an enterprisewide, yet common view of the impact of various sourcing relationships and of Multisourcing as a whole.

FIGURE 7-1

Hierarchy of value measures and outcomes

The figure shows the levels of value with the relevant impacts, or outcomes, sought at each level. As you climb each level, the business management responsibility for delivering outcomes increases while the service management responsibility decreases.

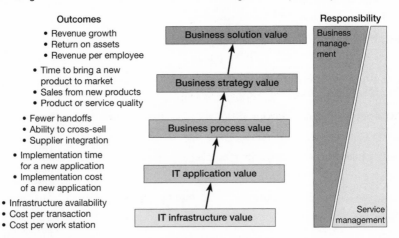

Source: Adapted from Marianne Broadbent and Ellen S. Kitzis, *The New CIO Leader* (Boston: Harvard Business School Press, 2005), 253.

Create a Hierarchy of Views

While this ability to provide an enterprisewide, top-to-bottom view is important, such a broad view is not useful on a day-to-day basis. It is better suited to quarterly reviews of Multisourcing management. Managers and executives do need daily information, though, on how all services are performing. This information needs to be filtered to include only the data of specific relevance. Otherwise, executives will miss all the important information while swimming in a sea of data.

Your dashboard should contain at least four specific viewpoints that separate the value measures on the basis of the target audience. In table 7-3, we show the four views that your dashboard should include, with a sample of the value measures that matter to each of the audiences.

By segmenting the audiences and filtering the data, you can provide for each level a unique view that hones in on what really matters from each audience member's perspective—and this targeted information will have much more impact in proving the value and success of Multisourcing. The amount of data presented at each of these viewpoints should differ as well. As you move from left to right in the table, the

TABLE 7-3

Multisourcing dashboard viewpoints and value measures

A dashboard should contain at least four views that segregate data on the basis of the priorities of the intended audience. The executive view should contain different measures from the service management view, for instance.

Service operations view	Service management view	Business unit view	Executive view
Service levels	Cost competitiveness	Market share	Top-line or bottom-line growth
Customer satisfaction	Efficiency	Time to market	Risk
Availability	Effectiveness	Forecasts	Return on investment
Utilization	Total cost of ownership	Cycle time	Innovation
	Portfolio analysis	Return on investment	Compliance

TABLE 7-4

A sample business unit dashboard

This dashboard is for a financial services company with locations throughout North America. The dashboard displays composite scores for each city as well as scores for the major processes for each city. The dashboard uses a traffic-signal metaphor with the colors red, yellow, and green. We have represented red as black, yellow as gray, and green as white.

	Customer service	Home loans	Bill payment	Application processing	City average
Atlanta	◐	○	○	●	○
Charlotte	○	○	●	○	○
Chicago	○	●	○	○	○
Cincinnati	○	○	○	○	○
Dallas	○	○	◐	○	○
Detroit	○	○	○	○	○
Kansas City	●	○	●	○	○
Los Angeles	○	○	○	●	○
Montreal	○	●	○	○	○
New York	○	○	●	○	○
Orlando	○	○	○	○	◐
Philadelphia	○	◐	●	○	○
Portland	○	○	○	○	○
Salt Lake City	●	○	●	○	○
Seattle	○	●	○	●	○
St. Louis	○	○	●	○	○
Toronto	○	○	○	○	○
Vancover	○	○	○	○	○
Overall result	○	○	○	○	○

● Problem
◐ Caution
○ Acceptable/meets expectations

dashboard for each target audience should display less and less raw data. So, for instance, table 7-4 displays a business unit dashboard that a client created. Note that it includes no raw data on service levels, customer satisfaction, or any other specific metric. The dashboard aggregates this data into a simple scheme (black, white, and gray) so that a quick scan can reveal any major issues. The business unit executive can then decide whether to spend time drilling down, rather than being forced to drill down on every point (a situation that would render the dashboard useless).

Now Back to the Beginning

As we've warned you several times, Multisourcing is a cyclical activity full of feedback loops and parallel efforts. The good news is that you will never run out of opportunities to practice your Multisourcing skills. The bad news is that you will never be finished with the process; when it is functioning properly, it is continuously refreshing itself as business needs, performance, capabilities, and other factors change.

All your measurement processes and dashboards need to feed back into the sourcing strategy process so that decisions can be revisited, evaluated, and revised as necessary. The combination of sourcing maxims, sourcing governance, the six comanagement processes, and solid sourcing measurement will minimize the impact of change—you will be more agile, more able to take advantage of new opportunities, more able to innovate for competitive differentiation. Multisourcing will allow you to move beyond outsourcing and its pitfalls, to find your way through the wilderness to the gold of business success that you knew was hidden there all along.

The Multisourcing Imperative

MULTISOURCING IS A REVOLUTION IN BUSINESS operations as dramatic as the industrial revolution and the advent of mass production a century ago. Just as we no longer remember those companies that were overwhelmed by the industrial revolution, two decades from now the companies that have not adopted Multisourcing will be either cautionary tales of failure to adapt to a changing world or simply forgotten.

It is not just a question of moving away from the vertically integrated corporate behemoths that ruled the first half of the twentieth century. It is a question of always, *always,* sourcing one's needed capabilities and competencies from the best possible mix of internal and external resources. Multisourcing is the culmination of a decade of thinking about what is core to the organization and the creation of a laserlike management focus on continuously improving those core functions and capabilities. As Ashwin Adarkar, CEO of IndyMac Bank's consumer bank and head of IndyMac's corporate development, says, "If

IndyMac Bank is to offer the best return to our shareholders, we must source highest-value services and talent on a global basis. There is tremendous value to be harnessed by embracing this opportunity." This is not a case of just saying the right things for public consumption. Adarkar notes, "Developing and executing on global sourcing is one of IndyMac's nine key strategic initiatives for the next year."[1] For most organizations, Multisourcing will require this level of attention from senior executives and boards of directors for the simple reason that change from traditional modes of operation is difficult.

Multisourcing is both science and art. The science, as we've tried to show throughout the book, involves definite frameworks and approaches that can guide you in developing and implementing a successful sourcing strategy. But Multisourcing also requires thoughtful management of relationships and people; resource decisions have a very real human face, and these decisions speak louder than words in creating the culture of an organization.

Change Is Not Optional

MULTISOURCING *will be* the new normal for successful business operations. By following the principles and practices of Multisourcing, you'll move beyond the pain of outsourcing to the successful sourcing of services from the most appropriate providers. You will integrate and manage those services successfully and provide your enterprise with the agility it needs to maximize growth opportunities.

Given the effort and discipline required to successfully implement a Multisourcing operational model, some companies may be tempted to simply wait, squeezing the last few dollars of benefit from outmoded approaches to outsourcing. These organizations might not attempt change until the processes are more standardized and sourcing competencies are more readily available. Unfortunately, waiting is not an option. The combined forces of core-competence focus, information technology, communications, globalization, and hypercompetition will not allow companies to stand pat in their current ways of operating. Multisourcing will be the dominant model of the future, and those companies that master it now will be positioned to lead their industries and drive competitors out of business. Those that refuse to change will constantly be operating at a disadvantage to competitors that are better able to focus management efforts, resources, and capital on the functions that deliver differentiation and value to customers.

The need to master Multisourcing is already being felt. Entrepreneurs will tell you that venture-capital firms are increasingly unwilling to fund start-ups that do not have a global sourcing strategy in place. Increasingly, investors and Wall Street analysts are insisting that a firm have a well-articulated plan for sourcing certain services externally. For a short while, expertise in Multisourcing will provide a competitive advantage. Soon, however, basic Multisourcing competence will be a requirement to stay in business. We are never going back to the days of vertical integration and the corporation as monolith.

Multisourcing today is clearly an opportunity to excel, to drive significant added value for customers and for shareholders, and to outstrip competitors. From basic IT services to complex business processes, your organization will draw its services and capabilities from a shifting blend of internal and external sources that serve the organization in meeting its goals for cost efficiency, agility, and growth. An organization's ability to recognize that its boundaries have fallen, that the corporate walls of yesterday have become porous and ever-shifting, will be a measure of its probability of success.

The reason it is imperative to adopt the discipline of Multisourcing now and move beyond outsourcing is that Multisourcing is not a goal in and of itself. Soon, you will have to have Multisourcing deeply ingrained in the organization so that you can again build on it not as the new focus but as the foundation for addressing significant changes in the ever-evolving business climate. Specifically there are three major trends (among many) that will require you to have mastered Multisourcing if you are to be able to respond to continuing market changes appropriately.

The Resource Crunch in the Industrialized World

Many governments and other organizations in the industrialized world are only now beginning to awaken to the realities of demographics. Every industrialized country is facing a population shift as the combined forces of increased longevity and slower population growth mean the average age of these societies is rising. Soon, the number of retirees in Western societies will skyrocket. Successive generations are not large enough to make up for the huge number of retirees who will be leaving the workforce. Since the mid-1990s, leading business strategists have been warning of a significant human capital resource crunch when this occurs. There will be massive competition for high-quality employees in industrialized nations; there simply will not be enough skilled and experienced employees to go around.

The facts of demographic change mean that organizations that want to thrive will have to be creative in their resource-acquisition strategies. Those that have embraced and mastered Multisourcing will be well ahead of the game in acquiring (on a global basis) the talent and expertise needed to survive the industrialized world's resource crunch. If you are just beginning to implement Multisourcing when the crunch hits, not only will you lose out on the best employees in the industrialized countries, but you'll also come in second in filling gaps with resources from other regions.

Redefining Boundaries

Ronald Coase won a Nobel prize in 1991 for work he had done in the 1930s attempting to define the boundaries of corporations: What dictated the optimal size of internal operations? In his remarkably prescient work, essentially foretelling the modern era of outsourcing, Coase concluded that a business would hire employees until the cost of managing them internally matched the cost of contracting for resources externally.[2] The dramatic declines in the costs of contracting for external resources, largely driven by technology advances, is the theoretical underpinning of outsourcing.

As the boundaries of the firm shrink and become more fluid, there are critical decisions to be made about where appropriate boundaries are. No longer is the question purely focused on costs; it also focuses on strategic issues. In March 2005, *BusinessWeek* ran a cover story on the growing practice of well-known companies outsourcing not only manufacturing but also product design, research and development, and innovation.[3] The article quotes Jim Andrew from The Boston Consulting Group about the dangers in these choices: "If the innovation starts residing in the suppliers, you could incrementalize yourself to the point that there isn't much left." Ed Zander, CEO of Motorola, is also quoted in the article and speaks about the importance of deciding what you hold on to: "You have to draw a line. [At Motorola] core intellectual property is above it, and commodity technology is below it."

This question of where the line is drawn will become increasingly central to business strategy, and perhaps even be the definitional responsibility of CEOs. Unfortunately, there will never be a foolproof way of drawing that line; only experience in drawing it and living with the consequences will be of substantial value. Organizations with a strong foundation of Multisourcing will have the advantage of experience drawing this line widely around the organization. Multisourcing organizations that try to figure out the answer to these questions of where the boundaries lie, without the benefit of years of multisourcing experience, will suffer.

Services Revolution

Finally, we must consider the services revolution, a concept pioneered by Uday Karmarkar, the *Los Angeles Times* professor of technology and strategy at the Anderson School of Management at the University of California—Los Angeles. In a June 2004 *Harvard Business Review* article and as a speaker at Gartner's Sourcing Summit in 2005, Karmarkar notes that the services industry has entered an era of intense competition.[4] He describes the era as similar to what occurred with U.S.-based manufacturing in the late 1970s and early 1980s. Today we marvel at how many manufacturers, particularly in the electronics and auto-manufacturing industries, were caught flat-footed when Japanese companies took the U.S. market by storm. Services industries will witness the same sudden need to rapidly improve their competitiveness in the face of global competition and the industrialization of services.

Organizations that embrace Multisourcing will be in a position to glean best practices and innovation in service delivery from their partners and apply it to their own business. They will have built deep pools of relationship-management experience that will translate into improved performance not just in operations but in a service company's core business. Organizations that do not have these networks of partners and pools of experience will be the losers in the services revolution.

Seize the Opportunity of Multisourcing

F RANCISCO CORONADO'S dismal reports of the American Southwest had far-reaching effects. Because of his dreadfully disappointing mission, the Spanish largely ignored the Southwest and did not invest in colonizing and developing California. Eventually, this lack of investment led to the ceding of the territory first to Mexico and then to the United States. The Spanish did not believe it worth the fight to hold on to these territories. Of course, today California's gross domestic product alone is several times larger than Spain's, not to mention the rest of the region. We see too many organizations that, running headlong into outsourcing, have encountered challenges and, rather than try new approaches, have retrenched or lowered their expectations. Just like the Spanish and Coronado, these organizations are in serious danger of missing tremendous value because they fail to adapt to new circumstances.

The new approach of Multisourcing is the answer to the challenges of outsourcing. Multisourcing can provide all the benefits we've discussed, and more. It can deliver unprecedented agility and growth. It can turn average organizations into world-beaters. But Multisourcing cannot do this overnight. As Barbara Scarcella notes, "Jumping in and trying to change how you approach sourcing all at once won't work. We had to look for low-hanging fruit, easy opportunities to deliver hard dollar benefits based on a common approach to existing sourcing problems. Once we had success to point to, we were able to build on that step-by-step."[5]

Throughout the book, we've returned to four key themes regarding strategy, governance, relationships, and effective measurement. While starting small is the right approach, set your sights high—drive these key themes into every part of the enterprise's culture. We've found that taking a different view of your sourcing relationships is often the hardest part of implementing Multisourcing. This view of relationships is summarized by Bill Oates, CIO of Starwood, "It's not about blame; it's about teamwork. We're really in the same boat with our partners, and the bottom line is it doesn't matter where the leak in the boat is. We're all going to go down if we can't solve the problem, if we can't deliver business value."[6]

Until everyone involved in service delivery shares this view of sourcing relationships, you'll struggle with Multisourcing. This is a great place to start your journey. Use the trust and control framework and other relationship evaluation tools in chapter 7 to assess your current internal and external sourcing relationships.[7] This process, along with your services map, should help you identify some of the low-hanging fruit that Barbara Scarcella refers to.

Implementing Multisourcing is not easy, but hundreds of organizations are beginning to implement Multisourcing and realizing bottom-line benefits. Your organization can join them and be ahead of the trends that will force change. There's a lot of work to do—so get started now.

Assess Your Management Capabilities

AS THE OLD ADAGE GOES, YOU CAN'T MANAGE WHAT you can't measure. One of the key parts of Multisourcing management is measurement. Most measurement in sourcing aims to evaluate the providers' performance. To master Multisourcing, you need to assess the quality and maturity of your management capabilities: Do you have the right mix of competencies working with the right processes based on the right data to make good day-to-day sourcing management decisions? Certainly, there are key markers of the outcomes delivered—positive sourcing outcomes indicate strong Multisourcing management. However, these typically long-term outcomes are lagging indicators of your management performance. For optimum performance, you need at the very least coincident, if not leading, indicators of your Multisourcing management performance. You need an idea of where to focus efforts for maximum impact.

This is the very advanced stage of Multisourcing management. Very few organizations have progressed to the stage of putting in place measurement processes for their governance and management of sourcing.

This is most definitely not the place to start. If you are just getting started in adopting the Multisourcing approach, creating strategy and defining and initiating your comanagement processes are a far higher priority. Only when you're well on the way to having these established should you devote considerable resources to this last element of Multisourcing management.

There are two aspects of assessing your Multisourcing management capabilities: management workstreams and indices for measuring performance.

Nine Multisourcing Management Workstreams

YOU CAN THINK of the nine Multisourcing management workstreams as horizontal workflows that fall within the Multisourcing management office. These responsibilities serve as the inputs to the comanagement processes. They are the behind-the-scenes work that must be done for comanagement to function correctly. Whereas the comanagement processes have separate instances for each managed relationship, the management workstreams are virtual representations of the common responsibilities across everything the management office does. The figure shows the nine workstreams in relation to the six comanagement processes. As you look through these workstreams, you must bear in mind where they reside in the organization and what they achieve. These workstreams manage the sourcing of services, not the services themselves. The workstreams that manage most of the services reside in operational areas elsewhere in the organization if you do not form a true Multisourcing management office.

- *Program management:* Maintains overall contract controls and monitors change over time. It focuses on managing the strategic and change activities related to service sourcing, covering both internal and external delivery sources in a sourcing portfolio. Program management provides visibility across projects and

FIGURE A-1

The nine workstreams of the Multisourcing management office

Three parties are involved in the management of service relationships: service consumers, the Multisourcing management office, and the service providers. The six comanagement processes, represented by the shaded bars, manage the relationships between the parties; the nine workstreams are the common and continuous management actions that feed the comanagement processes.

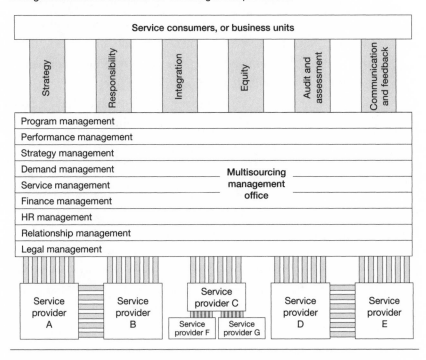

services and addresses the interdependencies among service providers.

- *Performance management*: Ensures adherence to performance standards and commits to improving performance. Performance management establishes the approach and processes to oversee how a service provider's performance matches the commitments in its service level agreements.

- *Strategy management*: Aligns sourcing and sourcing maxims with the company's business strategy. This workstream ensures that the delivery of services follows the defined business and sourcing strategies. Strategy management validates the sourcing business case and ensures that value measures of sourcing performance meet company value requirements.

- *Demand management:* Maintains a consistent approach and standardized processes for meeting the demands of service consumers. It focuses on customer satisfaction and ensures the adequate delivery of services to meet business unit needs. It does so through attentive management of customer priorities and adherence to reliable customer-delivery metrics. This workstream prioritizes customer requirements and manages the flow of demand from internal and external business sources.

- *Service management:* Ensures the successful delivery of contracted services. Service management oversees service delivery activities covering the service portfolio, from operational projects (support, maintenance, and problem management) to change projects (transfers, exits, and transition).

- *Finance management:* Addresses the financial implications of service delivery. This workstream focuses on the financial activities in the sourcing portfolio, such as service funding, pricing, internal chargebacks, financial assessments, and price and performance benchmarking. It ensures that the organization realizes all the financial implications of the sourcing contracts.

- *Human resources management:* Oversees the people-related issues and the processes resident in the sourcing management organization. It provides change management, training, and recruitment, and it manages the organization's competencies.

- *Relationship management:* Ensures that the organization and its service providers achieve the strategic objectives of their sourcing agreements while maintaining the long-term nature of their established sourcing relationship. This workstream measures the alignment of objectives, makes sure adequate relationship controls are in place, and drives the service relationships to achieve a balance between trust and control across all service providers and the company.

- *Legal management:* Oversees all sourcing-related contract development and contract administration activities. These include service-scope and delivery-model changes that may be required as a result of ongoing changes in the market, changes to the organization's business needs, and changes in technology. Legal management also identifies legal risks that may arise during the sourcing arrangement.

Again, these responsibilities of the Multisourcing management office allow it to effectively comanage. Without functioning finance and demand workstreams, for instance, equity comanagement will have faulty inputs and thus faulty outputs. You may wonder why there is not a procurement management category. Procurement is a discrete, point-in-time function rather than an ongoing one that is directed by legal management, finance management, service management, and so forth. Thus, procurement is not an insignificant activity but it is not a continuous workstream.

Five Indices for Measuring Performance

To CREATE coincident and leading indicators of the performance of the Multisourcing management office, you can score the performance in each of the nine workstreams along five factors.

People

You need to ask numerous questions about the human element when measuring your organization's performance in Multisourcing. For example, what is the level of investment in people associated with the responsibility? Do they have the requisite level of skills, training, competencies, and demonstrated effectiveness? Is the infrastructure in place to support the ongoing needs for competencies in this area? Here are some potential responses to these questions:

- *No support:* There is no specific investment in people or skills.

- *Minimal support for people and skills:* Competency acquisition, measurement, and training are ad hoc.

- *Moderate support for people and skills:* There is formal competency acquisition and training, but this support is underfunded.

- *Enhanced support for people and skills:* Competency acquisition and measurement are proactively managed.

- *Optimal support for people and skills:* Competencies in this responsibility are continuously improved and are measured as best-in-class.

Process

In answering the question "What is the current level of process maturity in this responsibility?" most organizations will have one of the following responses:

- No process exists.

- Policies and processes are defined.

- Policies are enforced.

- Streamlined policies are enforced.

- Continuous improvement is in place.

Technology

Various enterprises use technology to different extents in their Multisourcing management office. To what extent has technology been adopted for the fulfillment of the office's responsibilities?

- *Chaotic:* There is little to no use of technology.

- *Reactive:* Technology use is limited to responding to ad hoc requests.

- *Proactive:* Technology use is consistent in supporting this process.

- *Service:* Technology supports this process through defined measures.

- *Value:* Technology is optimized to support, align, and meet business objectives.

Investment

What is the current level of financial investment and funding to enhance the performance of the responsibility?

- *None:* Performance is being allowed to degrade.

- *Minimal:* There is stopgap investment.

- *Maintenance:* Investment is only enough to maintain current performance; performance relative to peers may be degrading.

- *Enhanced:* There is proactive investment to improve performance.

- *Optimal:* There is continuous investment in improving performance.

Confidence

Multisourcing relies on relationships, which require trust and confidence. Balancing trust and control is a key element of service evaluation that we cover in chapter 7. Here you are evaluating the management office's ability to create trust and confidence in both service consumers and service providers.

- *None:* The parties in the relationship have no confidence and see no value in the Multisourcing management office; parties avoid interactions with this office.

- *Adversarial:* The parties engage in the relationship but view the Multisourcing management office as an adversary.

- *Neutral:* The Multisourcing management office is viewed as neither helpful nor unhelpful.

- *Positive:* The parties believe that the Multisourcing management office can help achieve outcomes.

- *Partner:* The parties are strongly committed to working together through the management office procedures.

- *Comanagement:* The parties understand, implement, and value the comanagement processes and the role of the Multisourcing management office.

Synthesizing an In-Depth View

B Y SCORING EACH of the nine horizontal workstreams against these five indices, you can get an in-depth view of your capability to successfully perform in a given area. This will also help you prioritize your efforts for the development and improvement of your sourcing management capabilities. Quantitative measures of management are only possible once outcomes are determined, but these qualitative measures allow you to predict future success. If you have the right people, processes, and use of technology and the appropriate levels of investment, you can have great confidence that your sourcing management will be effective at delivering the expected outcomes, even as those expectations change. If, on the other hand, you are deficient in any of these areas, you can expect your performance to suffer.

Notes

Introduction

1. For details on the impact of outsourcing on valuations, see Vijay Gurbaxani and Philippe Jorion, "The Value of IT Outsourcing Arrangements: An Event Study Analysis," working paper, Center for Research on IT and Organizations, The Paul Merage School of Business, University of California, Irvine, May 2005. For details on the impact of outsourcing on CEO compensation, see Andrew Stein, "Study: CEOs rewarded for outsourcing," CNN/Money, http://money.cnn.com/2004/08/31/news/economy/outsourcing_pay/.

2. Dick LeFave, CIO, Nextel, e-mail correspondence with authors, February 2005.

3. Bob Ridout, CIO, DuPont and Maryann Holloway, director, IT Alliance, DuPont, telephone interview with authors, March 10, 2005.

4. Some consider Eastman Kodak's 1989 contract with Digital, IBM, and others the advent of modern commercial outsourcing, which led to fundamental changes in attitudes about the sourcing of services. Others consider the founding of ADP in the 1940s the start of modern outsourcing.

5. Forecast growth based on Dataquest market research on the services industry. For more information, see www.gartner.com.

6. Minor details of each of these stories have been changed to protect the confidentiality of clients.

Chapter 1

1. Members of his party were the first Europeans to see the Grand Canyon. They were not impressed: the party estimated that the Colorado River, which was flowing at

the bottom of the canyon and which today supplies most of the water to Southern California, was only eight feet wide.

2. Perhaps worse, Coronado's unrelentingly dismal reports on the value of the American Southwest to Spain directly influenced the Spanish colony in Mexico to cease the exploration of the western United States or any attempts to colonize it. Thus, when the growing United States seized what was called the Territory of California from Mexico in the 1800s, Mexico was unable to defend its territory. In another bitter irony, Mexico ceded California to the United States mere months before gold was discovered near San Francisco in a discovery that set off the famous 1849 gold rush. For more information, see Marc Reisner, *Cadillac Desert* (New York: Penguin, 1993).

3. Partha Iyengar, Fran Karamouzis, and Ian Marriott contributed to the development of our view of global sourcing options.

4. Chris Ambrose, Roger Cox, and William Maurer helped develop the management and measurement implications of the three types of deals.

Chapter 2

1. The material presented here on sourcing strategy is based on the work of Claudio Da Rold, among others.

2. The management-by-maxims process was first researched and described by Marianne Broadbent and Peter Weill. A fuller description of it can be found in Marianne Broadbent and Peter Weill, "Management by Maxims: How Business and IT Managers Can Create IT Infrastructures," *Sloan Management Review* 38 no. 3 (Spring 1997): 77–92; Peter Weill and Marianne Broadbent, *Leveraging the New Infrastructure: How Market Leaders Capitalize on Information Technology* (Boston: Harvard Business School Press, 1998); and Marianne Broadbent and Ellen Kitzis, *The New CIO Leader: Setting the Agenda and Delivering Results* (Boston: Harvard Business School Press, 2005).

3. Matt Arnold, principal, Unimax, telephone interview with authors, December 8, 2004.

4. Mark Nelson, executive vice president, Global Resources, IndyMac Bank, telephone interview with authors, March 31, 2005.

Chapter 3

1. Research by Claudio Da Rold, Cassio Dreyfus, Doron Cohen, and Jeremy Grigg contributed greatly to the development of the material we present here on sourcing action plans.

2. Francisco D'Souza, chief operating officer, Cognizant Technology Solutions, e-mail correspondence with authors, March 2005.

3. Mark Nelson, executive vice president, Global Reources, IndyMac Bank, telephone interview with authors, March 31, 2005.

4. The sourcing models presented here were originally detailed by Claudio Da Rold.

5. The material presented on business cases for sourcing is largely the result of work conducted by Arnoud Klerkx.

Chapter 4

1. Cassio Dreyfus has led much of Gartner's research into the successful governance of sourcing. The material presented here is based on Cassio's recent research.

2. Bert Liverance, director, Global IT Operations, Nike, telephone interview with authors, March 29, 2005.

3. Dick LeFave, chief information officer, Nextel, e-mail correspondence with authors, March 2005.

4. Some highly service-specific roles may also need to be retained. For instance, in IT, many organizations choose to retain a role called *technology advancement,* which focuses on exploring emerging technologies and possible applications to persistent business problems.

5. For more information on the Feeny-Willcocks model, see David Feeny and Leslie Willcocks, "Core IS Capabilities for Exploiting Information Technology," *Sloan Management Review* 39, no. 3 (spring 1998): 9–21.

6. The principles of comanagement were originally developed by Roger Cox and elaborated by Cox, along with Ronan O'Mahoney, Gerwin Pol, and Martin Stacey.

Chapter 5

1. Brian Keane, CEO, Keane, Inc., e-mail correspondence with authors, March 2005.

2. The Fast Track process was developed in an effort led by Chris Campbell, Lorrie Scardino, and Denise Underwood. Specifically, Underwood applied her considerable experience in implementing the Fast Track process in assisting us with this chapter.

3. The material presented here on SoWs and SLAs is based on the work of Bill Maurer and Rich Matlus.

Chapter 6

1. We acknowledge the help of Bill Maurer, Kevin Parikh, and Denise Underwood, specifically their in-depth experience with sourcing contract negotiation, in the development of this chapter.

Chapter 7

1. For more information on the captain's log and other fascinating aspects of navigation before the invention of the maritime clock, see Dava Sobel, *Longitude* (New York: Penguin, 1996); and Mike Dash, *Batavia's Graveyard* (New York: Crown, 2002).

2. The trust and control framework was developed by Roger Cox.

3. The material presented on sourcing dashboards is based on the work of Chris Ambrose, Phil Georgas, Bill Maurer, and Denise Underwood.

Conclusion

1. Ashwin Adarkar, CEO, Consumer Bank, IndyMac Bank, e-mail correspondence with authors, March 2005.

2. The costs of employees that Coase referred to were management and resource allocation costs. The costs of contracting for resources included researching options, negotiating, writing and managing contracts, and enforcing contracts. For more information on Coase's Law, see his paper, "The Nature of the Firm," http://people.bu.edu/vaguirre/courses/bu332/nature_firm.pdf.

3. Pete Engardino and Bruce Einhorn, "Outsourcing Innovation," *BusinessWeek*, March 21, 2005, 84–94.

4. Uday Karmarkar, "Will You Survive the Services Revolution?" *Harvard Business Review*, June 2004.

5. Barbara Scarcella, Strategic Sourcing Office, Thomson, panel discussion, Gartner Outsourcing Summit 2005, Los Angeles, CA, April 5, 2005.

6. Bill Oates, chief information officer, Starwood, panel discussion, Gartner Outsourcing Summit 2005, Los Angeles, CA, April 5, 2005.

7. Also available online at www.gartnerpress.com/multisourcing.

Index

access quadrant in four worlds of
sourcing model, 27. See also four
worlds of sourcing
Adarkar, Ashwin, 215
analytical hierarchy process (AHP),
175–176, 177f
Andrew, Jim, 219
Arnold, Matt, 48
audit and assessment comanagement
process, 136–137

Basel II, 70
best-of-breed consortia sourcing option,
94–95
branded services, 93
building a sourcing strategy
customization decision, 75–78
defining outcomes in business terms,
69–70
determining scope of services to be
aggregated, 73
financial considerations (*see* financial
considerations in outsourcing)

four worlds overview, 74, 75f
internal vs. external sourcing (*see*
internal or external sourcing
decision)
key questions overview, 66–67
location dependency decision (*see*
location of services)
map creation, 107–109
map update, 73
matching outcomes to deal type, 71–73
nonfinancial factors, 106–107
problem of specifying the process over
the outcome, 67–69
service outcome statements examples,
71
standardization costs and benefits,
77–78
build sourcing action, 92
business case components
cash flow and variable costs, 106
cost categories to consider, 101–102,
105t
costs estimates for options, 103,
105–106

business maxims. *See also* maxims;
    sourcing maxims
  articulating for sourcing strategy
    preparation, 52–54
  categories of, 54
  converting to sourcing maxims, 59t
  using to create sourcing maxims,
    55–57
business outcome achievement
    framework, 168
business outcomes, determining
  define outcomes in business terms,
    69–70
  determine scope of services to be
    aggregated, 73
  matching outcomes to deal type,
    71–73
  problem of specifying the process over
    the outcome, 67–69
  service outcome statements examples,
    71
business strategy
  comanagement process and, 133–134
  governance and, 112
  sourcing models (*see* service value and
    delivery)
  sourcing strategy preparation and, 40,
    44–45
buy sourcing action
  best-of-breed consortia, 96
  full-service outsourcing, 93–94, 95
  prime contractor, 95
  selective outsourcing, 97

call centers, 6
capability maturity model (CMM), 183
Capgemini, 98–99
captain's log, 193
captive offshore services, 24. *See also*
    nondomestic sourcing
Champy, James, 5
chief sourcing officer, 62–63
China, 23

CMM (capability maturity model), 183
Coase, Ronald, 218
comanagement
  audit and assessment, 136–137
  communication and feedback, 137
  creating in an existing relationship,
    135
  equity, 136
  implementing, 140–141
  integration, 135–136
  managing change, 138–140
  overview, 132, 133f
  relationship with management roles,
    137, 138t
  responsibility, 134
  strategy, 133–134
  value of, 128, 131–132
communication and feedback
  comanagement process and, 137
  gauging community reaction to
    outsourcing, 48–51
  miscommunication when outsourcing
    services, 8
  strategy planning need, 151–153
competency center, 117–118
compete sourcing action, 92–93
confidence
  as an index for measuring
    performance, 229–230
  trust and (*see* trust in a relationship)
contracts
  negotiation and (*see* negotiation in
    sourcing deals)
  relationships in sourcing and, 200
  terms and conditions in provider
    packet, 157–159
cooperate sourcing option, 21–22, 97.
    See also joint ventures
"Core Competence of the Corporation,
    The," 5
core competency of a company, 5, 88
Coronado, Francisco, 17–18, 19, 220
cost of services. *See* financial
    considerations in outsourcing

cost-plus pricing, 167
Covisint, 28
creation quadrant in four worlds of
    sourcing model, 28. *See also* four
    worlds of sourcing

dashboards
    definition and purpose in
        Multisourcing, 209
    hierarchy of views, 211, 212t, 213
    linking value measures, 209–210
deals, sourcing
    efficiency, 29, 30–31, 167, 168
    enhancement, 29, 31–32, 167, 168
    matching outcomes to, 71–73
    transformation, 29, 32, 168
    types, 29–32
    weighting of criteria, 178f
D'Souza, Francisco, 68
DuPont, 4, 126, 128, 130f

efficiency sourcing deal
    described, 29, 30–31
    pricing frameworks for, 167, 168
enhancement sourcing deal
    described, 29, 31–32
    pricing frameworks for enhancement
        deals, 167, 168
Entergy, 72
enterprise-level sourcing governance,
    60–64
equity comanagement process, 136
evaluating and selecting service
        providers
    crafting win-win-win relationships,
        144, 145
    Fast Track process (*see* Fast Track
        process)
    myth of the enemy, 11, 143–144
    offshore providers, 183–186
    sole-source alternative, 147–148
    traditional RFP evaluations, 146–147

evaluation team, building
    gathering and updating inputs,
        154–155
    interaction plan specifications,
        155–156
    membership, 153–154
exit plan, 168–169

farmshore sourcing, 23
Fast Track process
    building an evaluation team, 153–156
    communication plan importance,
        151–153
    creating a provider packet (*see*
        provider packet creation)
    described, 148–149
    governance and, 150
    government organizations and, 150
    negotiation and (*see* negotiation in
        sourcing deals)
    phases overview, 151
    selection process (*see* selecting a
        provider)
fee-for-service pricing, 167
Feeny-Willcocks model, 126
fee reductions, 162–163
financial considerations in outsourcing
    cash flow and variable costs, 106
    circular nature of process, 100–101
    cost categories, 101–102, 105t
    costs estimates for options, 103,
        105–106
    elements of business case for
        sourcing, 101–103
    financial engineering and, 104
    internal vs. external sourcing costs, 86
    pricing frameworks for deals, 167–168
financial engineering, 104
fixed price, 167
four worlds of sourcing. *See also* service
        value and delivery
    cost considerations with
        customization, 75

four worlds of sourcing (*continued*)
  customization decision, 77–78
  governance and change management
    limitations, 75–76
  integration of the new services, 76
  overview, 74, 75f
frameworks, pricing, 167–168
full-service sourcing option, 93–94, 95

geopolitical risk-management, 82–83
global delivery model, 24
Global Resources group, IndyMac Bank,
    128
governance
  critical nature of, 14, 113–115
  described, 112–113
  enterprise-level, 60–64
  failure problems when outsourcing,
    8–9
  Fast Track process to selection and,
    150
  importance to business strategy, 112
  of management functions (*see*
    management of sourcing)
  markers of good governance, 115–116
  maxims and (*see* sourcing maxims)
  measuring progress (*see* measuring
    progress and performance)
  statement of work, 164–165
government organizations and Fast Track
    approach, 150

Hamel, Gary, 5, 88
Hammer, Michael, 5
Harrington, Richard, 63
Health Insurance Portability and
    Accountability Act (HIPAA), 70
Holloway, Maryann, 4
human capital assets
  building a sourcing strategy and,
    79–80, 86–87
  evaluating competencies, 45–46, 47

location of services considerations,
    79–80
people as an index for measuring
    performance, 227–228
statement of work and, 165–166

incentives, 162–163
India, 23
IndyMac Bank, 50, 51, 83–84, 128,
    129f, 152, 185, 216
innovation workshops, 180
integration comanagement process,
    135–136
internal delivery sourcing option, 91–92
internal discovery process
  business strategy, initiatives, and
    competitive stance, 44–45
  human capital assets, 45–46, 47
  knowledge capital, 46–48
  organizational communications and
    politics, 48–51, 151–153
  risk tolerance, 51–52
internal or external sourcing decision,
    89f
  benchmarking, 87–88
  competence and differentiation
    evaluation, 88–90
  human capital assets and, 86–87
  physical and knowledge assets and, 87
  service costs, 86
  service level needed, 85–86
  sourcing relationships and (*see*
    relationships in sourcing)
investment as an index for measuring
    performance, 229

joint ventures, 97, 98–99
Jones, Chris, 94, 95

Karmarkar, Uday, 219
Keane, Brian, 145

knowledge capital
  internal discovery process, 46–48
  internal vs. external sourcing decision
    and, 88
  knowledge transfer and location of
    services, 81

LeFave, Dick, 3, 123
Liverance, Bert, 121–122
location of services
  captive offshore services, 24
  evaluating an offshore provider,
    183–186
  geopolitical risk-management need,
    82–83
  integration complexity and
    dependencies, 83–84
  knowledge transfer, 81
  nondomestic sourcing, 23
  people intensiveness/human capital
    required, 79–80
  relationship requirements, 80–81
  security and control, 81–82

management of sourcing
  benefits from active management,
    12–13, 121–122, 220
  capabilities assessment, 224–230
  functions, 116–117
  governance in Multisourcing (see
    governance)
  management office implementation,
    117–118
  management office role, 118–120
  organizational roles, 127–128,
    129–130f
  role profile for provider management,
    126f
  roles and needed competencies,
    122–123, 124–127
  roles that can't be outsourced,
    123–124

service coordination (see
  comanagement)
management quadrant in four worlds of
  sourcing model, 26–27. See also
  four worlds of sourcing
manufacturing outsourcing, 2
mapping out Multisourcing
  four worlds of sourcing, 75f (see also
    service value and delivery)
  global sourcing options, 23–24
  map updating, 73, 107–109
  service delivery options, 24
  services map example, 33–34
  sourcing actions, 21–22
  types of sourcing relationships, 29–32
  types of value delivered (see service
    value and delivery)
maxims
  ability to connect strategies, 42–44
  aligning with governance, 60–64
  for business (see business maxims)
  description and purpose, 41–42, 53
  for sourcing (see sourcing maxims)
  starting with internal discovery (see
    internal discovery process)
  strategy vs., 43
McNealy, Scott, 63
measuring progress and performance
  dashboards and (see dashboards)
  evaluation phases, 196–197
  indices for, 227–230
  ineffective practices, 194–195
  price measurement, 198
  relationship measures (see relationship
    performance assessment)
  service level measurement, 197–198
  value measurement, 198–199
Multisourcing
  ad hoc outsourcing vs., 19
  benefits from active management,
    12–13, 121–122, 220
  as a business imperative, 215–217
  definition and scope, 1, 3–4, 19–20
  key themes, 14–15

Multisourcing (*continued*)
　major trends, 218–220
　mapping (*see* mapping out
　　Multisourcing)
　measuring progress (*see* measuring
　　progress and performance)
myth of the enemy, 11, 143–144
myths of outsourcing of services, 10–12

nearshore sourcing, 23
negotiation in sourcing deals
　long-term viability of the vendor and,
　　189
　strategy for, 188, 190–191
　team members for, 187–188
Nelson, Mark, 50–51, 84
New Horizon System Solutions, 98–99
Nike, 121–122
nondomestic sourcing
　captive vs. outsourced services and,
　　23
　choosing service location and (*see*
　　location of services)
　evaluating an offshore provider,
　　183–186
　global delivery model and, 24
　global sourcing options mapping, 23–24
　"offshoring" vs. "outsourcing," 79
　relationships to offshore sourcing, 23

Oates, Bill, 221
offshore sourcing. *See* nondomestic
　sourcing
Ontario Power Generation (OPG), 98–99
optimization quadrant in four worlds of
　sourcing model, 27–28. *See also*
　four worlds of sourcing
organizational communications and
　politics, 48–51, 151–153
outsourcing of services
　analogy to Coronado, 18

business changes requiring a new
　approach, 18–19
compulsive outsourcing, 6–7
definition and scope, 2
factors influencing spread of, 5–6
governance failure problem, 8–9
miscommunication problem, 8
myths of, 10–12
new strategic approach to (*see*
　Multisourcing)
poor coordination problem, 9–10
success of, 1–2

people as an index for measuring
　performance, 227–228
performance of a provider. *See*
　measuring progress and
　performance
Prahalad, C. K., 5, 88
pricing frameworks, 167–168. *See also*
　financial considerations in
　outsourcing
prime-contractor sourcing option, 94–95
private utility, 77
process as an index for measuring
　performance, 228
provider packet creation. *See also*
　selecting a provider
　contract terms and conditions,
　　157–159
　enterprise objectives, 157
　exit plan, 168–169
　governance statement of work,
　　164–165
　human resources statement of work,
　　165–166
　pricing, 167–168
　services statement of work (*see*
　　services statement of work)

Qualex, 94–95

Reengineering the Corporation, 5
Reiner, Dietmar, 99
Reisner, Marc, 18
relationship performance assessment
   alignment and vision and, 200
   contract terms and, 200
   customer service, 199–200
   prioritized evaluation criteria use, 199
   trust and (*see* trust in a relationship)
relationships in sourcing
   assembling choices, 98–99
   comanagement process for existing,
     135
   crafting win-win-win, 144, 145
   insourcing option: branded-services,
     93
   insourcing option: internal delivery,
     91–92
   insourcing option: shared services, 92
   location dependency decision and,
     80–81
   options overview, 90–91, 91f
   outsourcing option: best-of-breed
     consortia, 94–95
   outsourcing option: full-service,
     93–94, 95
   outsourcing option: joint venture, 97,
     98–99
   outsourcing option: prime contractor,
     94–95
   outsourcing option: selective
     outsourcing, 96–97
   performance assessment (*see*
     relationship performance
     assessment)
   verifying, 136–137
responsibility comanagement process,
   134
Reusch, Grant, 63
RFP evaluations, 146–147
Ridout, Bob, 4
risk tolerance
   considering in a strategy, 51–52, 107

geopolitical risk-management need,
   82–83
shared-risk/reward pricing, 168

Salesforce.com, 28
Sarbanes-Oxley Act, 70
Scarcella, Barbara, 63, 220
scoring system, 179
selecting a provider. *See also* provider
   packet creation
   choosing providers to participate,
     172–175
   conduct due diligence, 181–182
   evaluate responses, 179–180
   evaluating an offshore provider,
     183–186
   evaluation model creation, 175–179
   oral interviews, 179–180
   scoring system, 179
selective outsourcing option, 96–97
service level agreements (SLAs),
   160–161, 162t
service outcome statements, 71
service provider selection. *See* evaluating
   and selecting service providers; Fast
   Track process; provider packet
   creation; selecting a provider
services outsourcing. *See* outsourcing of
   services
services revolution, 219–220
services statement of work
   incentives and fee reductions,
     162–163
   innovation, 164
   measurement, 161–162
   roles and responsibilities, 159–160
   scope of the work, 159
   service level required, 160–161, 162t
   transition, 163
service value and delivery
   benefits of categorizing services, 28
   business models for sourcing, 26–28

service value and delivery (*continued*)
  categorizing a service based on its
     value, 25–26
  standardization vs. customization, 26
shared-risk/reward pricing, 168
shared services sourcing option, 92
SLAs (service level agreements),
     160–161, 162t
sole-source evaluations, 147–148
sourcing maxims. *See also* business
     maxims; maxims
  aligning business and IT strategies,
     60, 61
  aligning with governance, 60
  business maxims used to create,
     55–57
  creating, 57–60
  deriving from business maxims, 59t
sourcing strategy
  business vs. sourcing strategy, 38
  importance to business strategy, 14,
     40
  misaligned strategies examples, 35–37
  misalignment due to disconnected
     business and sourcing strategies,
     40–41
  misalignment due to no sourcing
     strategy, 38–40
  for negotiation, 188, 190–191
  preparation for (*see* sourcing strategy
     preparation)
sourcing strategy preparation
  enterprise-level governance, 60–64
  internal discovery process (*see* internal
     discovery process)
  maxims for (*see* business maxims)
  understanding sourcing options,
     55–57

SoW (statements of work)
  governance, 164–165
  human resources statement of work,
     165–166
  for services (*see* services statement of
     work)
strategy. *See* business strategy; sourcing
     strategy

technology as an index for measuring
     performance, 228–229
traditional RFP evaluations, 146–147
transformation sourcing deal
  described, 29, 32
  pricing frameworks for, 168
tribal knowledge, 48
trust in a relationship
  components of, 203t
  confidence levels and, 203, 205
  control and, 204t
  importance of, 201–202
  scoring a confidence index, 202–203,
     205
  situations that disrupt confidence,
     206–207
  using to repair a relationship,
     207–208

value of a service. *See* service value and
     delivery

workstreams, management, 224–227

Zander, Ed, 219

About the Authors

Linda Cohen is a managing vice president in Gartner Research, where she leads the Gartner Strategic Sourcing practice, providing life-cycle support to clients procuring or delivering strategic sourcing services. Before this position, she served as research director in the area of external service providers and as primary research director in the areas of IT consulting, systems integration, and outsourcing. Ms. Cohen has more than twenty years of experience in IT management and outsourcing. Before joining Gartner, Ms. Cohen worked for a large IT services vendor in various management positions, ranging from program director of outsourcing operations to outsourcing marketing director in both government and commercial markets.

Allie Young is a vice president in Gartner Research, where she is part of the IT Services and Sourcing team. Since joining Gartner in 1990, she has focused her research on the broad developments in outsourcing, monitoring key market trends, competitive issues and provider strategies, user outsourcing requirements, outsourcing contract issues, and the impact of new delivery models and global sourcing models on buyers and providers of services. She also contributes to Gartner's applications-outsourcing and global-sourcing research communities. Before joining Gartner, Ms. Young worked independently as a market research consultant. Ms. Young received a bachelor of arts degree from Gustavus Adolphus College in English/Literature.